1,134 Days to 0

Triumph over $37,000 of Debt in Three Years, One Month

Heather DeVito

WESTBOW
PRESS

A DIVISION OF THOMAS NELSON

WestBow Press books may be ordered through booksellers or by contacting:

WestBow Press
A Division of Thomas Nelson
1663 Liberty Drive
Bloomington, IN 47403
www.westbowpress.com
1-(866) 928-1240

ISBN: 978-1-4908-0186-5 (sc)
ISBN: 978-1-4908-0185-8 (hc)
ISBN: 978-1-4908-0187-2 (e)

Library of Congress Control Number: 2013912618

Printed in the United States of America.

WestBow Press rev. date: 7/25/2013

Madeline and Bethany, this book is for you. You are the light of my life; my two beautiful daughters for without you my world would be empty.

I also dedicate this book to my brother Gregg, my best friend who left this earth far too soon and much too young.

The following people have either been my foundation, my strength through the years, or my support throughout the process of this book:

God

Mom

Donald DeVito

Kurt & MaryBeth Miller

Chris & Janina Miller

Gregg Miller

My father

Paul & Lucy Hoffmann

Cherise Kramer

Matt Roe

Jean DeVito

Debbie Rexine

I'd never have gotten through this without the support of the most awesome friends a girl could ever hope for:

Christina (Chuckie) Breun

Debbie Rexine

Vanessa Baggett

Patti boomba-latti Thomas

Sandy Marji

Janina Miller

Nancy Corvo

That leaves Josh. What can I say about my Joshy? I put up with you, you put up with me. Who knows, maybe that's what makes us work. I truly appreciate how much you waste fruit. The day I looked out the back door and saw the oranges in the snow, I knew I had the cover for my book. Thank you for your endless support, words of encouragement, and belief in me when I didn't believe in myself…but, don't *ever* run my dishwasher…

This last note is a "pre" thank you to Andy Cohen from Bravo TV for inviting me on his show. As soon as I'm sitting in the Clubhouse, I'll know I have arrived!

The Menu

Prologue

I'm going to run right out of the gate. No sense in wasting time because time is money and money pays the bills. I simply decided to write this book because I was excited about my recent accomplishment and extremely proud of myself for setting out to complete a challenging, long-term goal. It took a lot of patience and even more sacrifice to feel what the results of being debt-free would bring.

I'm going to let you know how I did this, not by listing numbered "chapters" or a list of how to's. Though if you pay attention, by the end you will know how to. I'm taking a different approach and going in my own direction. I've read several books out there that are supposed to give you the information to better your life, improve your future, yadda, yadda, yadda, and I just never seem to get anything out of them. Except that by buying the book, I have bettered the author's life. Good for them. If their book sells then they succeed, but unfortunately we're still stuck here trying to figure it out.

I'm going to share my personal experiences and stories. If you really read them and hear them, you will find them chock full of hints and ideas. I lead by examples of what to and what not to do, descripted by the mistakes I've made and the times I've been fortunate to get it right. I've made enough mistakes to go around and I'll let you in on them so you can avoid them or stop making them going forward.

I am not looking to make a million dollars, though I do aspire to be successful. If this book gets published, it means I wrote it and my success has already begun. If it becomes a financial success, then that's the cherry. I can still have the sundae if I don't become a gazillionaire or NY Times best seller. The accomplishment is not in how much money you make, though it helps to make good money. It starts with setting a realistic goal and working at it until you accomplish it.

Will I feel more successful if it becomes a best seller? Of course, but for now I'll settle for getting it bound and shipped, even if I have to sell them from the trunk of my car. The more difficult the challenge, the more rewarding the achievement will be. If everything were easy, why would anyone strive to be better? What would it be worth if everyone could have it all, without having to put the effort in to earn it? I wanted to write a book. If I achieve that goal, that is success in itself; If someone else gets to read it then that's all the better. I'm no expert on finances. I'm just sharing what worked for me and incorporating a few stories in the meantime to show you how.

I did it by relying on myself, the most reliable person I know, though I've been known to let myself down a time or two. I can't say I did it without any outside assistance, because I'd be nowhere right now without the biggest influence in my life, God, whom I thank every night and throughout the day, every day whenever any little thing goes my way. Of course there's also my boss for employing me. I reward him back with hard work and great production. We both like it that way.

I'm scared to proceed to the next step. I've never been so close to attaining my goals and achieving what I set out to do. I've faced so many obstacles and jumped so many hurdles along the way, I find myself looking all around me before I pull into traffic or cross the street because I wonder if I'm going to get hit by a bus. How could life be getting so much better? I have to believe this is what reaping the benefits of hard work is. I earned this and as scary as it seems, it feels good, and maybe I even deserve it.

I'm still reeling from what I've accomplished. I'm not saying I've found the cure for a rare disease, or made a great life accomplishment, but it's important to me and it's important that I do the best I can for my girls while teaching them from my mistakes. I did what so many people wish they could do. For whatever reason, they can't get out from under the mountain of bills that never get delivered to the wrong address like their favorite magazine. It's common sense. Spend less than you make. The hard part is living it, sticking to it, and having the patience to see it through to the end. You can believe me, not because I'm telling you, but because you can do it too!

Come join me in the time of yesteryear where we lived within our means, not by everyone else's standards or by keeping up with appearance.

I guarantee the appearance isn't that pretty when the door closes at night and you can't sleep because you don't know how you're going to pay for something you couldn't afford.

As I was saying, I was really proud of myself. I couldn't help but tell everyone I knew which is entirely different than when I had an embarrassing amount of debt. Anyone who knows me knows I am actually a very responsible person. My ex-husband even suggested I title the book, "Frugal Chic" which almost caused me to fall out of my chair laughing. Getting in debt happened, but it couldn't continue. I had to get my head above water and I started by reaching for the surface. I didn't think about how much it totaled. I kept plugging along keeping my eye on the prize. This is not a race for the hare; this is a race for the tortoise and we know how that story turned out. It doesn't apply all the time but it does apply here. My problem didn't happen overnight and I wasn't going to snap my fingers or wiggle my nose to make it disappear. This was going to be a long road.

I didn't realize until last week - when for a moment I began to think back to three years ago when I started to tackle the balances and chop them down - what it amounted to. Looking back, I had forgotten several credit cards that were long paid off because they were smaller and first on the list. I paid a lot more than I originally realized.

No one brags about having bad credit or being over their heads in debt. We're supposed to pretend that we're getting along just fine. Well, I wasn't getting along. I was simply surviving, and barely. I was living paycheck to paycheck in a new apartment and on my own for the first time in eight years.

Now that we have the basic introductions out of the way, I'll explain briefly why I have the gall to believe what I have to say warrants your time to read. I believe I have information you will find useful, delivered in layman's terms that can be understood because I am just like you.

I am your normal every day, average American making a lot less than the experts who write these books, and keep repeating themselves throughout the entire book, not offering an iota of sustenance. Thank goodness I've only wasted a little money on a few of the many books available, and I didn't fall into the trap of paying for any expensive seminars. Half way through these books I wonder when the writer is going to say something that may be useful or pertinent to solving a problem, or answer the question they keep promising to answer from cover to cover. I'm not going to deliver anything other than my story.

I made a decision that was easy enough to make and simple enough to follow, but really hard to stick to. You can't eliminate debt without the proper tools. You'll need to make a budget, accept sacrifice, and you're going to need discipline. You're going to need all three of those things but especially the discipline, because without it, you'll get nowhere.

You'll learn how you can still have what you need and just a bit of what you want. Eventually you can have it all - just not until you pay for what you already have.

I'll explain from 'soup to nuts' just how crazy I am… crazy enough to make it work!

Place Your Order

Taxes

I wondered if I would have enough to say to fill an entire book, but who was I kidding, I never shut up! You will probably get through this book in a few days. I am going to be jumping around but in the end, I'll tie it all back together in what I like to think of as a nice, neat little present. A gift of how to change the way you live enough to have a profound impact on how you see, use and spend money.

Either way, I can't expect to help you get out of debt by having you spend more money so I'd like to go with a $12 price tag for this book. I figure $12 is a fair price because if you're in hot water with your credit cards you already have more to worry about than $12. In the end, this is a sensible investment because it'll be the best $12 you will ever spend. Twelve dollars, not $10, because it's shiny. The two or three people in the world that know what the heck that last statement means will laugh. I'll explain it to the rest of you later in the book.

I am not smarter than anyone else. I completed several semesters of college at a few different schools but without a degree because I didn't finish.

I know how to balance a checkbook and I know how to make and stick to one heck of a mean budget. I can stretch a nickel into twenty dollars and I will tell you how. Don't confuse this with a book about how to make money. If I knew how to do that I wouldn't have to worry as much about being in debt. I say I wouldn't have to worry *as much* because having more money doesn't mean you don't need to worry about debt. I know enough people who make a lot more money that I do, and all they have is bigger debt. Just look at the celebrities that had millions of dollars but still spent more than they earned and had to file for bankruptcy.

I speak in past tense about being debt because last week I made the final payment on the last credit card I still owed on from when I was married. The grand total was $37,500. I did it in three years, one month. I was a little late reaching my goal by one month because Uncle Sam won't let me file my taxes in December.

I had the e-mail with all of the figures (except my W-2) typed up and ready to send to my accountant sitting in my draft folder by December 15. I knew what expenses I would be deducting. I added up my receipts and went on-line to find whatever interest I could deduct, and got a pretty close estimate of my daycare expenses.

Before I go any further I would like to get something straight. I am not by any means proud of amassing that amount of debt. I am more than embarrassed by it but I can't change the past. I can only change my habits and what I do in the future so I will not be in that position again. I accepted my mistakes, owned them and embraced a way to get out of it.

In fact, the biggest slap in the face I received was a typical comment that came from my mother. She came to visit just a few days after I set up the final on-line payment to US Bank. We use the same accountant and the subject of taxes came up during dinner. I told her I had already received my refund and had just paid off the last of my debt.

After she asked me if I have anything left from the refund (I didn't), I was **still** trying to feel proud of myself and foolishly revealed just how much I had paid off in three years' time.

I was beaming at my $37,500 accomplishment, and so then came the pat on the back. Wait for it....drum roll....wait for it....

She said, "You know what would have been even better than that?" I dared to ask, "What?" She responded, "Not having that debt to pay off in the first place."

Bam! So there you have it folks, the accolades from a proud parent *who's never been in debt before.*

I thought you'd get a kick out that. I did. In fact, I emailed that to my ex-husband. He's witnessed the relationship dynamic I have with my mother and I knew he would understand. He was saddened by her comment but I told him that the best feeling I could get would be when I put that quote in my book.

What could be a better motivator for me than success? I printed what I wrote in the email to my ex-husband Daniel, cut it out and stuck in on my fridge. I read it every day just in case I was too tired to type one night. It was like rocket fuel.

Tax time is my favorite time of year! I didn't think I could love or appreciate anything more than Christmas, but boy I am like a kid on Christmas morning for two to three months before tax time. I work my way through the entire year just to get to tax season.

I let the government use my money, although I'm probably better at budgeting than them right now, seeing as they can't stop spending long enough to get our country out of debt. Talk about setting a bad example! Maybe some folks in Washington ought to read this book.

[Sidebar: Our state and local government could use an overhaul in common sense. Every year I receive a packet of forms in the mail that I am required to fill out and return. It is the free lunch application for my children at their public school. It costs money to employ a whole slew of people to type and print them, money to mail them, and a return envelope is included with postage paid. The packet comes to both my house and my ex-husband's. With our incomes our children are never eligible for free lunch. I think that what it must cost to send this packet to every single household for each child attending school is more than redundant. If they took the money that the applications cost to print, mail and process, they'd probably have enough money in the budget to offer free or reduced lunch to everyone.]

I didn't have the discipline to file head of household with dependents to get the extra money in my paycheck. It's the first step to learning a discipline that you don't currently have. If you give it to Uncle Sam to borrow, you are forced to learn to live without because he takes it before you can get your hands on it and waste it.

I know the CPA's are gritting their teeth at the idea, but if I had the discipline to invest that money myself throughout the year and not use it then I wouldn't have had $37,500 of debt to pay back. So I give the government the opportunity to make money on my hard earned income, and in return my reward is one fat lump sum check that I immediately use to pay off as many bills as I can. Then I *never* use those accounts again, with the exception of the two major credit cards I save for emergencies and to keep my credit established.

I have written a whole book on how to erase debt. I have even included pictures of some of the crazy things I do to stay on budget and make the most out of every penny that comes through my checking account.

I'm going to get on my high horse now and then, go off on what seems to be a useless tangent, but there is something for everyone in this book that is bound to help you learn to fix the mess you have put yourselves in.

I could have easily decided to write a book about bad relationships but I haven't figured out how to fix those yet. I'll stick to what I know, which is paying bills. I enjoy paying bills. I hate to see my money disappear, but I get such a physical sense of relief when I check my account balance and have enough money to pay them. Gone are the embarrassing phone calls from collection agencies or the notices that come in an array colors in my mailbox notifying anyone who processes the mail that I am behind on my bills.

So you're in debt. Who's not? I've been told only one percent of Americans are debt-free. I'll also bet that half of that one percent is only debt free because they've already destroyed their credit so badly that they aren't eligible for any, and they don't own anything because it's been charged off or written off in bankruptcy. I'd also bet that they are probably pretty dissatisfied with life, though they'll never admit it.

These are the people who always complain that life stinks and that it is from no doing of their own. If you are one of the people who swears that you're doing everything in your power to get it right and it's not going right because of everything and everyone in the world except you, then you should read this book a few times.

I'm going to start my little book by saying the very same thing I have read in every other instructional book, self-help book, money management guide, etc. that I've read thus far.

This book will be different from any other book you've ever read, but that's where the similarities end. I promise.

My book is different because I don't have a college degree. I'm not an executive business woman who is a finance guru trading stocks in the finance district or giving seminars on how to improve your life. I am a very hard-working single mom of two beautiful little girls and I have nothing more than discipline, drive, and common sense.

Stop reading right here if you don't have the patience it's going to take to fix a problem that crept up over time. Instant results won't be found here; you'll have to look elsewhere if that is what you seek. I'm not going to tell you how get rich quick or at all. I am not rich. I am debt-free, and ready to begin the next chapter of my life.

Who knows, I might follow up with another book about what success I grab next. You can guarantee that my tremendous goals are divided into a few smaller goals. As I complete each, on I go to conquer the next.

I am talking about smaller goals like skipping spending money on lunch one day. I'm talking about day-to-day changes that force you to do something to fix your money problems with nothing but sheer determination and desire. Doing a little bit every day for as long as it takes, making a huge impact in the end.

You won't understand the magnitude of what I've just said until I delve in to the "how" with my stories. I'll detail the unorthodox approaches I took to get where I am. You may think it's crazy. I can all but guarantee that. What I do sometimes is lunacy but it works.

This book will help you with many things, but for the most part it is just a story about a 34 year-old stay-at-home mom, turned insurance agent that had been walking around for days asking people if she looked different.

When they asked if it was my hair, my make-up or my outfit, I would say, "No".

I looked different because I just become one of the *one percent* of America that is debt-free. I didn't walk away and let someone else foot the bill – I earned it.

I look different now because the stress has been eased and I'm no longer burdened with the weight of the world on my shoulders. Actually I still worry, because if I don't, then something might happen that I'm not prepared for. Now what I don't worry about are my bills.

Let's get back to the taxes. In 2011, I filed my 2010 taxes and received a whopping $7500 back. I no longer have a house, mortgage interest, property taxes or anything else to claim as deductions. I claim only my two daughters and the daycare expense for one of them because Daniel and I split the daycare. We each pay for one child. I can't use his tax receipt as a daycare expense so even though it's a complete waste that goes unused.

I wouldn't dare tell Uncle Sam I paid for something that I hadn't because I don't want to face the dreaded *audit*. I get whacked with 33.5% every other pay period and the government owes me that money because I truly am in the 27.5% bracket.

When I received this tax return via direct deposit, I immediately paid off the $1900 Macy's balance, which was $2700 the year before. I had stopped using it and just kept plugging away with as much as I could pay each month. By the time tax season was upon us, it was $1900. I choose direct deposit for my tax returns because I get my refund back weeks faster than if I wait for a check.

In the meantime, I had also paid off a pesky Home Depot bill and the balance on my Discover Card, which was about $2500. I paid all three of those bills in full. I keep doing this, living with so much less of my paycheck than I should because it is on loan to the US Government, but this is what works for me.

By the time tax season came around again in 2012, I was making a significantly larger amount of money, though still in the 27.5% tax bracket. I'm not even close to reaching the next rung of tax responsibility, but because I made more I was taxed more.

I absolutely hated that US Bank took $214 out of my checking account on the day of their choosing, anytime between the 14th and the 19th of every month. I agreed to it because they gave me a 5.99% interest rate for 60 months for doing it. I always just deducted it from the check-book register on the 5th and forgot about it. I wasn't going to play Russian roulette with my checkbook wondering if this month they would take it on the 20th which was the next payday.

In 2012, when I filed for the tax year of 2011, I received a mammoth $9800 back from my new favorite uncle, Sam. I started making my list of eligible debt pay-off months in advance. It was so motivating to see the results of my sacrifice so quickly approaching and I knew exactly how much I needed to fully pay said balances. If there wasn't going to be enough to pay something in full, then I allocated the funds for several smaller bills and started moving those payments to the bigger balances after the smaller ones were done.

My $9800 tax return paid off my student loan of $6600, and the entire Capital One balance was down to $2900 from the original $3500. I also made the last of a twelve-month auto loan payment, freeing up $458 per month.

At that point there was no way to consider placing that chunk on the US Bank balance because it was still over $8500. That one would have to wait.

I used my Capital One card and my State Farm Visa throughout the year for purchases that I had held off on for as long as I could but needed, and I was careful to be mindful of my balances. I paid off the balances every month and since I was used to saving as much as I could for an Aruba trip (I'll explain about that later), I kept saving. By summer I had amassed over $5000 in savings and only owed on my US Bank bill in addition my normal monthly expenses.

I kept on trucking throughout the year, and before I knew it by September I had my Capital One card debt back up in the $1800-2000 range. I was continuing to make $500-600 payments each month, but the balance was creeping up. I still hadn't learned my lesson.

I loosened the purse strings a little and although it didn't become a full-blown free-for-all, I was coming dangerously close to going right back to where I started. The savings I put away that I told you about? I couldn't even begin to tell you where it went. I know I spent some on my daughter's birthday party in the summer -she finally got the American Girl Doll she had for three years been asking for - but you can say it was wasted, and I was secretly embarrassed.

Here comes tax time again. This year was going to hurt because technically it would be Daniel's year to claim both girls, giving me no deductions. However, I negotiated with him to allow me to take one child as a deduction and he wouldn't have to repay money I loaned to him earlier in the year.

I am a really cool ex-wife, but when it comes down to the nitty-gritty, I can be very *persuasive*. He gets one child this year along with the taxes, mortgage interest, etc., for a house that is still in both of our names, so it wasn't entirely unfair for me to request having one little deduction. We both benefited from that negotiation.

Again, by mid-December, 2012 I had all of my paperwork in the draft folder of my Outlook raring to go to the accountant as soon as I had my W-2 and could click send. The dilemma this year was that the old Bush tax cuts expired and the software wasn't ready for filing, so no one could file until January 31!

My accountant e-filed for me on January 31, 2013 and by February 8 I had my federal refund direct deposit of $7487 in my account. I was still waiting for NY but I'm always waiting for NY. I file early because I made the mistake ONCE of filing at the end of February and by the time my refund was processed NY ran out of money and froze all returns until they received the money from people who owed. That will not happen again if I can help it. I got a total of $8400 back this year, because I lost the rest giving it to Daniel. We get along really well though, so in some cases, very rare cases, money isn't everything. Giving him that child tax credit was going to help him, and in turn, it would help my children. It was well worth it.

February 8, 2013

I couldn't sleep. I awoke at 2:33am on February 8 and thought, why not just check to see if the deposit is there in the pending section? I got on-line and sure enough, my money was there!

KeyBank is so awesome about deposits and other transactions. They don't put ridiculous holds on my funds. I've banked with them long enough to know that pending on the 8th means cleared on the 9th. I had my money! The 9th was a Saturday though. I immediately went on-line and set up a payment for Monday just to be safe that the money would be cleared, and I completely paid off that last balance to US Bank. I had reduced the balance to $5998.05 after three years of paying $214 every month. Reminder: the balance when I started with the automatic payments was $10,600 in August of 2010.

I was so excited that I got on the phone with US Bank at 2:35 in the morning and said, "Stop the automatic payment on the 15th! I just paid the balance in full!" Then I started yelling, "Yay Me!"

The guy on the other end was so cool. He was congratulating me and I was laughing as I explained that I've been waiting to pay this off for so long that I couldn't wait until the morning.

He had to transfer me to the credit card department, but that was ok, because I excitedly yelled the same thing into the phone to that guy! I was on a roll. I told him how I couldn't sleep so I thought I'd check for my deposit and it was there and now here I was talking to him. Everyone got such a kick out it. I bet so many people never pay these balances off, but I did!

I had to make one more phone call in the morning. My payments were managed by the "hardship department" and only they could stop my payments. The hardship department wasn't open at 2:35am, only customer service for regular customers.

I went through the entire account for the third time with her on the phone, but there was such a difference in her tone when she took my call. This was a customer service rep that was different from the two previous reps I had the pleasure of speaking with.

This girl worked in the department where people didn't pay their bills. Her tone started with just the right touch of disdain that I could come to expect from the hardship department, but I didn't let it get me down. I told her I paid my balance with the same enthusiasm I told the first two reps, only with slightly more hesitation like a little child waiting to be patted on the back. Well guess what? She lightened up very quickly because my happy spirit was too infectious for even her to ignore. She too got on the Heather train of kudos, kudos all around!

I changed her opinion of just one "hardship case" today. I paid off a balance that was previously getting ready for charge-off or collections or worse, judgment.

She even felt bad when she had to tell me that she could see my payment of $5998.05 scheduled for Monday, but that unfortunately that balance didn't include this month's interest. In order to really pay that balance down to $0 I had to give her another $36.26.

Yup. I didn't even know what else to say to her. I offered to pay it then and there and then joked asking if she was going to charge me a fee to pay it over the phone. She laughed and told me no, no fee. She got a kick out me.

The automatic payments have now stopped and that account reflects a $0 balance. The next morning I put another chunk onto the Capital One card that was starting to get me back in hot water and also paid off my State Farm Visa completely. That's the end of my credit card debt…again.

I was able to do it because I loaned the Federal Government my money and because I now live a completely different lifestyle. I may not have to loan that money to my Uncle Sam anymore. I'm not sure what I'm going to do going forward. I think I may let him use it for one more year, because when I get my ten thousand dollar refund next year, I can plunk it down on a house. I'll keep you posted.

In the meantime, I'll start putting everything I was paying on those accounts into a savings account to add to my tax return and it will be completely possible for me to have fifteen to twenty thousand in cash on hand for buying a house. I'm getting a little ahead of myself here, so I'm going to go in reverse a little and tell you how I got here, and how I worked for three years, one month to get out of it.

Bread

The start of the meal

The next sentence is in bold because it's an important one.

I had to accept that incurring this debt was of my own doing with no one else to blame, and I decided that it also needed to be of my own undoing.

I was going to be providing for my children and I couldn't let them down. Of course I would succeed; they were counting on me. Failure was not an option. I'm the mommy, and the mommy has to do it. The daddy does it too, for all you fathers out there, but this is my story and in it, I am the mommy. I had to repeat it to myself to give myself the strength and courage to forge on some days. I am not talking about affirmations in the mirror. You won't catch me doing that. I earn my affirmations from those who see what I am doing and from my own success. I feel affirmations. Saying them in mirror isn't my thing but hey if that works for you, then have at it.

Taking the easy way out wasn't an option so the thought of filing bankruptcy NEVER crossed my mind. This didn't happen overnight. It took years of doing the right thing, really doing the right thing, before things started to shift. Slowly at first, but then they snowballed.

Daniel and I were newly married and broke with our first daughter in diapers. He was able to put his ego aside and allow me to take the lead with the finances. Magically, I managed to get everything paid - and on time! The hard pill to swallow, though, was that there was never anything left over. Daniel hated that after I paid the bills I left us with nothing.

We dined at a $5.95 per person Chinese buffet on discount night down the street from our apartment once a week for our night-life. We rented two dollar movies on special. Every time we rented our third movie, we got a free rental next time. That two dollars stayed in the account and got added to the three dollars I saved somewhere else, so when I needed to get milk before payday, it was there. It wasn't bad. Believe it or not, we were happy. There was screaming and fighting over most everything else, but it almost always somehow revolved around money.

I must admit that while we dated we made the foolish mistake of never discussing where each of us got our money from, how we budgeted or what we were saving.

Make sure you know ahead of time what your partner's spending habits are. What are their views on money, finances, the future, and who is going to control the finances? Yes, I mean control the finances (not the relationship) because that's the only way it will work - with control.

If you can't agree, don't mix the money! I've never understood how that works, and I don't believe it really can work. How can one spendthrift save and be responsible if the other party can't budget and winds up constantly hitting up the other to bail them out? You're still going to fight unless there is a lot of compromise. You can also consider keeping three accounts. One account for each that is separate, and the third specifically for bills, but you'd better have direct deposit into that account and only the more responsible person should have control over it.

I didn't even know that he was behind on the child support for his two sons until after we got married and an awful lot of our wedding money went to pay it current. I cringed at writing those checks. I didn't begrudge the boys their money. It was owed to them and it was due. Boy did that open my eyes really fast and give me more than a glimpse of what the future would hold if it didn't get corrected, fast. I was ticked, and the honeymoon was over.

That was gift money from our families to start our future, and a sizeable chunk of it went to paying for the past (bills I mean, not the kids). I immediately stepped in and spent the first solid year of our marriage writing letters disputing his credit reports and amending incorrectly filed tax returns. I diligently worked to get our credit in order because I was going to own a home if it killed me.

Daniel saw the fruits of his labor in little ways and I managed to keep us fed with steak once a week, diapers, fresh fruit, etc. on a forty dollar weekly budget. That's how my grocery sport began. I call it a sport because it requires immense concentration and determination but is really so rewarding, like solving the NY Times crossword puzzle.

I'm going to include a picture of the mess that becomes my grocery list so you can see how I am able to get every item I need, and come within pennies of what I have budgeted and estimated the bill to be. I did this for many years, but over time we had a little more.

If I look back to try to figure out where it all started, I'd have to say it started with American Express. At the advice of a financially successful family member, we applied for the AMEX. The idea behind her suggestion was that we should stop paying bills from our checking. Using our own money didn't give us reward points or cash back. We were supposed use this card to pay any and every bill that would accept American Express. We would then take the money we would have paid it with from our checking and pay the card back.

If we paid the balance in full every month the way AMEX required you to, we would also stop paying interest on our purchases. We were earning airline miles to get tickets for my step-sons to visit from New Mexico. It worked out pretty well at first. I didn't spend any more than we could afford to pay and our credit standing with American Express was so good that they continually waived the ninety-five dollar annual fee on our platinum card. Our standing was so great they sent us an offer we (meaning me) couldn't refuse. Any single purchase we made over two hundred dollars no longer needed to be paid in full at the end of the statement period. Wow! We were fancy! By then paying the bill was starting to become a struggle anyway, so guess what I started doing? Being the absolute genius that I was, any purchase I made that came even remotely close to two hundred dollars got bumped up. There were times I would have only spent fifty friggin' dollars for one purchase but bought more stuff to get my purchase over the two hundred dollar threshold. I know. I know hindsight is 20/20.

I still feel like a moron admitting that I did this. I am so smart yet fell into one of the dumbest traps I have seen to date.

Guess what happens when you make a payment on-line at 11pm on the due date because you forgot to pay it before 3pm? It posts the next business day, as the fine print tells you at the bottom of the payment screen. Then you get bumped to the default penalty rate of 27.99%. It's like prime plus 18%. I don't recall exactly because it was eight years ago. You also lose all of the points you've earned that statement period. The rules of the program state that in order to be eligible to receive the points you earn each statement period, you have to be in good standing on your account. There is also the $39 late fee to contend with because the payment was technically late. Don't worry, though. If you lose your points they let you buy them back for some ridiculous amount of money. We never did get to earn a free flight for the boys, either.

I'm not trying to bash American Express or require the need to retain counsel because they don't like what I'm saying here. It was my fault. They sent me a ton of paperwork outlining the terms and conditions, the rules of the program, etc., and I didn't read them. I got myself into hot water accepting an offer that was put on the table, knowing full well I had no business accepting it. It was like tempting a kid with candy. I shouldn't have done it, but I did. I played Russian roulette with that card and I lost.

I'd walk into a store at any given moment and walk out with $300 worth of crap I didn't need. I did this several times a week sometimes. I was trying to fill a void but it didn't work. Daniel was sometimes the culprit and before we knew it, we were in trouble and things were already not going well.

We were doing "ok" financially, meaning that with both of us bringing home a paycheck we were still able to cover our bills. It was a struggle most times though because we spent too much. I loath wasting money, or time for that matter, or energy, or really just wasting anything at all. It burns me up. I controlled the purse strings, paid all of the bills, and kept the budget on balance as best as I could during our marriage.

Daniel has been quoted as saying, "If it weren't for Heather, we'd have never owned a house; I don't know how she does it". It was a very frustrating balancing act trying to manage a checking account where two people each had a debit card linked to the same account. You can imagine what a nightmare that turned out to be. I spent what felt like an eternity sometimes just entering the debits. Neither of us ever carried cash on us. Cash just burns a hole in my pocket and makes me look for something to buy that I wouldn't have if I didn't have the money with me.

You'd be amazed at how fast and how much 10-15, two and three dollar purchases can add up to. I would sit down at the computer to pay the bills and balance the checkbook, knowing how much I needed to cover everything. I would sometimes spend hours just entering all of the debit purchases into the checkbook fighting back tears of frustration. I knew that when I finally got the total, there wouldn't be enough. I appreciated the challenge, though. Give me a challenge and I will rise to create a solution. When I got the remaining money figured out, I'd almost always find a way to make it work. I'd cut back on groceries or skip shopping for food altogether to make up for the shortage to be sure other bills were paid. We could make do with what was in the cabinets for a few more days or so. No one was going to starve.

I am not going to get hit with a late fee for not paying a bill, though, so those always get paid first. Under no circumstances, no siree Bob, no fun stuff or unnecessary purchases of any kind until all the money for bills is accounted for.

This may be one of the reasons I have often been referred to as "The fun police".

My husband and I had gotten ourselves into a bit of a pickle and I decided that we needed to get out of it.

At least I needed to get myself out of it. Sometime down the road I made one of the saddest and most difficult decisions I've ever had to make, and that was to end my marriage. Let me be clear. This was not a hasty decision, nor one that I took lightly. I am a firm believer in the institution of marriage. Besides that fact, the situation was ultimately a death of sorts, and I also had to figure out if I could do it on my own, with just my income.

Worrying about whether or not I could afford to stand on my own was not a reason for me to stay in an unhealthy environment, but it also wasn't a decision to rush into. If you rush and don't have a plan, you'll fall on your face. When I say unhealthy, I don't mean unsafe. We just didn't agree on anything anymore. Daniel and I had the same goals, but very different ideas of how to reach them, and we were setting a bad example for the children of what a loving family should be.

Now you may be wondering what the heck me telling you about the demise of my marriage has to do with getting out of debt, but through my experiences, you'll find the keys to your solution, and I explain them through story and examples. Maybe you will even relate to a few of them.

This brings me back to Daniel and the double debit cards linked to a joint account. It won't work if someone is drawing off the same account and only sometimes remembers to tell you that they used it, or once in a while gives you a random receipt. That was the end of the two debit cards for us.

I pride my ex-husband for his willingness to go along with that because sometimes pride and ego get in the way. With either of us it's hard for our dominant personalities to give up control. He was the primary bread winner and felt like he was working just to hand over his paycheck. I appreciated that this was one fight we didn't have to have. He didn't want to take care of the finances anyway.

Since I paid the bills and did the shopping I had to keep the debit card. If he needed money, he would come to me and ask for the card, followed by the question of how much he could take. Now bear in mind this was not my trying to control what he spent (who am I kidding, yes it was).

Daniel likes to eat out and as a Leo, feels that he more than deserves to do so. Why shouldn't he feel deserving? He works hard all day and needs to reap the rewards for his hard work.

What Daniel failed to accept at the time, is that he had a lot of fun throughout his twenties and into most of his thirties. I was guilty of that, too but I didn't have any children at the time. It was time to grow up and accept that a family relied on him to provide. It was a harsh reality, and there needed to be significant adjustments to how the money was spent. It was a hard pill to swallow. This may be something that you may need to take a look at. There is plenty of time for fun later. Get your chores done first.

The time came. I had to stop shopping. I hit a brick wall, and got slapped in the face with a very uncompassionate dose of reality. My marriage was really over.

Appetizer

Moving out

It was the difficult decision of opting to give my girls, our girls, two happy, healthy homes where they were loved and cherished, instead of one home with too many disagreements and not enough compromise or communication. Having the OCD personality that I do, I decided I would move out leaving the house to Daniel. I wanted this new start to be on my terms and that wouldn't have happened if I was going to wait for him to go, and I wasn't interested in fighting with him over a house.

In November of 2009 I secured an apartment and took up residence on the first of December. I'm giving you that specific date because that was the first day I took control of my new life and got started. I developed a budget, and very rarely waiver from it. Daniel and I agreed that we would each be responsible for any debt that was in our name. By that point, we had each secured two of almost every card - two Home Depot Cards, two State Farm Visas, and a few others. I took on the Macys card because it was in my name. He was taking on the mortgage and the HELOC because he was keeping the house. I took the minivan because he had his car. We covered every nook and cranny. Don't get me wrong, it wasn't easy and it wasn't always a pleasant conversation but we managed to get through it relatively painlessly.

I did not want a long, expensive, messy divorce, so I secured an attorney through a recommendation I received. He told me that if there was nothing to fight about, then I could expect to have everything completed for about twenty-five hundred dollars. How I managed to come up with the retainer is still beyond me, but like I always say there is money for whatever you want it to be for.

The expression that there is no such thing as a friendly divorce does not pertain to Daniel and me. We were determined get through it as cordially as possible. After all, we would have to deal with each other for the next twenty years since we are still connected by the children. I had no interest in fighting with him for those twenty years and we both wanted to set the best example we could for the girls considering the circumstances, and I was done fighting.

I gave Daniel the house, along with both the mortgage and the HELOC payment. I figured if he was going to regain the equity for a sale on the property later, then I had no obligation to continue paying on either bill. He did not have to buy me out, and I was not asking for child support. You heard me correctly. I did not request child support. In fact, my attorney all but called me crazy. I had to sign special documents formalizing it, because he was convinced that, "no judge in the land would sign off on my terms, thinking I had a gun to my head". My attorney said, "I was giving away the farm." I didn't care.

Truthfully, Daniel was never very good at sending out the bills - I told you about our wedding money - so I didn't want to come to rely on money that may or may not show up, and sporadically at best. I also didn't want to have to justify where my next pair of shoes came from; I didn't want to hear that child support was paying for my "lavish" lifestyle.

Along with everything else, Daniel is also entitled to claim both girls every third tax year. We have joint custody and I didn't feel like dragging him through the mud. He has the girls almost as much as I do, and I am just not the person who could request alimony. If I was going to start over, I was going to do it on my own without having to worry about being questioned about how I spent money if it wasn't all coming from just my income.

I can't comprehend why so many people spend a fortune on dragging out divorce, which is painful enough to begin with, just to squabble over minor details. Salvaging what was left of our relationship was far more important to me than making him suffer any further financially. Besides, in my opinion, unless you've been married for a really long time, I don't believe that anyone deserves to take half of what the other party has, or have access to future wages and pensions unless you grew those assets together. If you both started from scratch with nothing and built an empire together then go get what's yours. Daniel and I didn't have anything that was worth fighting over.

With that said, we started Daniel's 401K from scratch together. We both agreed to split it when we separated. I didn't even take half. He gave me a handsome check for $10,000 of what was in his $44,000 account and I went away quietly. I guess I know now where my retainer came from. The rest of the money immediately went to pay off as many balances as it could, and regretfully, I was more than generous with Christmas presents that year since the money came two weeks before that holiday.

My ex-husband and I get along extremely well. We have our occasional moments from time to time when we still squabble, but we truly get along better now than we ever did when we were married. He is my work out partner. We spend a few holidays together from time to time, and we go out to dinner with the girls on a somewhat regular basis. I say this to you because it might seem I paint an unfair picture of him throughout this book when I use him as my scapegoat. In reality he is no different than anyone else struggling to stay afloat. The divorce was finalized for the sum of $2900 and I don't know many people who can say they managed that while being able to split assets and agree on custody terms. I love Daniel. I always will. We just couldn't be married anymore. We are a family whether together or separate that is better all-around for how we handled ourselves.

Our children are very well adjusted because we treat each other with mutual respect. We have set an awesome example for them. Just because circumstances don't always work out the way we hope or plan doesn't mean it has to be a disaster.

One of the things I negotiated was taking the car. He had a car in his own name, and I wanted the mini-van because it was paid off. It was in his name, so he signed the title over to me. That title didn't actually get signed over until next spring though.

The van was getting up in mileage and I was driving over twenty miles each way to work. It was a top of the line version of Town & Country, with leather interior heated seats, electric sliding side doors and electric rear lift gate. I know every van comes with that now, but this van was a 2001 and the bumper-to-bumper extended warranty had already paid $2700 for a new transmission. It was fast-approaching 140K in miles and I was getting nervous that if I didn't replace it soon, I'd have nothing worth selling if I needed a newer car.

When it got really cold out, one of the sliding doors wouldn't work properly, the seat heat on the driver's side stopped working altogether, and little things were starting to go. The warranty on the car was long gone and it wasn't financially feasible to spend another $2000 on an extended warranty. It made sense the first time, but it was obvious that I still had a great car that would bring good, sturdy transportation to someone else that did less driving. If I was going to sell it, now was the time.

One of the reasons I am always able to get top dollar for my cars and practically drive them for free while I own them is because I keep very good files on everything. The car gets its own file and you can imagine the delight on a prospective buyer's face when I can produce the receipt for every oil change, brake change, rotor replacement, tie rod, or sway bar link.

When I tell them that the car was properly maintained they don't have to take my word for it because I have the paperwork to prove it. That is money in the bank. I can haggle with someone much better when they want me to drop the price because I pull out my magic folder and show them what a solid purchase they are making.

I am also very honest and tell them why I'm selling it. I told the couple that bought the mini-van that I drive too far to rely on it anymore. I knew that they only did very local driving for the most part. I explained how it still had plenty of trips to Pennsylvania left and was a good solid car, but after all the money I had put into it thus far, I wanted to sell it before anything major went wrong. I went on to tell them that the engine may have 140K on it but I have the paperwork for the brand new transmission that only has 65K. If something were to go wrong with the car after I sold it, I can rest in the knowledge that I didn't hoodwink anyone.

I bought a newer car for several good reasons. I say newer because only when I was really young and foolish did I buy cars new. One day a client called my office inquiring about insurance. His father-in-law had recently passed away and my client needed to get his car from North Carolina to New York. Over the course of our conversation I learned the car was rarely driven. It was garaged and had never seen salt or snow. Anyone from Central New York knows what salt does to a car! His mother-in-law didn't want the car after her husband passed away and was giving it to him to sell, so they could pay off some debt.

The car was a 2001 Buick LeSabre Limited and also had everything electric, leather interior, and included On-Star. The difference was that it only had 38K in miles on it. That was unheard of. I asked if I could buy it from him after I blue-booked the value and saw it was still worth almost $6500 in its current condition.

I told him I could give him $4000 but no more than that and he was pretty happy with it since to him it was just free money. He didn't have to take the time to wait for another buyer. He even changed the oil, put new tires on it for me and had it detailed. Score!

Although my credit wasn't entirely shot, State Farm didn't really want to give me a loan either. I called a supervisor and begged for a twelve-month loan and got it approved at 13.89%. I do not recommend anyone having that interest rate for a loan, but I didn't have a choice. I wrote myself a State Farm vehicle loan for $5000. That's our minimum loan, and figured I'd immediately take the extra $1,000 and apply it to the first two payments. The loan was going to be $458 per month for twelve months and I wanted to get a jump on it.

I could have shopped the rate but I make commission on the loans and insurance I write so it wasn't a total bust. At the same time, I brokered a deal with some friends of mine. Their car recently died. The transmission wouldn't shift past second gear and they couldn't drive over 25 miles per hour. They had Reverse when the car felt like cooperating. They were interested in my minivan. I didn't exactly like the idea of selling a car to a friend, but it in the end it worked out. They drive the mini-van to Ohio every summer and I still see her driving it in the morning when we drop our kids off at the same school. They bought it from me in March of 2009 and that van is still going.

Daniel and I paid $12,600 for that van back in May of 2005. We drove it for four years, and it was barely worth $6000 right now. I was going to try to sell it for $5500 if I could get it.

My friends couldn't get a loan because their credit was far worse than mine, but offered to make payments to me with interest. I did one better. I told them that I would sell it to them for $5700 with payments of $250 per month with no interest.

Originally they wanted to pay me $300 per month but I refused. I told them that I'd rather have them make a payment that they could handle rather than something that would come sporadically or late and that $250 seemed more reasonable. They agreed.

Technically I made more this way than if I sold it for less and took the interest. Daniel got $500 off the top from the down payment, in order to get him to sign the title over. I used the $250 payments I received to offset the overwhelming $458 payments I had to make to State Farm for the next twelve months.

The best thing about this scenario was that after I struggled through my loan and paid it off, not only did I have an installment loan on my credit report paid in full on time to bump my score, their payments continued for almost another year.

We paid $12,600 for that van back in 2005, drove it for over four years and I sold it for $5,700. It was almost like getting half my money back.

I still have my LeSabre and it's now 2013. Its book value just hits the $5,000 mark and I am now selling it for $4,500. Remember, I only paid $4,000 for it. I got to drive the car for three and a half years and sell it for more than I paid for it.

One mistake I did make was that I never took the extra thousand dollars from the LeSabre loan to use for the first two payments. I went to visit friends on Long Island which is where I'm from and before I could even see it happen, I blew the money on living the high life for a weekend at the best places. Clicquot champagne was flowing and everyone had a good time. So I'm not perfect. I completely screw up sometimes, and that one took a long time to recover from. Even after I got out the financial hump it caused, I mentally kicked my butt for quite a few more months. Nobody is ever harder on me than I am on myself.

I bought another used car last August for two or three really bad reasons. State Farm lowered their interest rates on vehicle loans and I was seeing applications for clients being approved left and right.

I was curious to see how two and a half years of my paying bills on time and paying some debt off had improved my credit rating. My youngest daughter had inquired on a few occasions as to when we would be buying a new car. The comments that an idiot I had interviewed for a job with were still lingering in the back of my mind. Those were not good reasons to go and buy another car, but I caved and just to see how I rated, I applied for another State Farm loan.

I was approved at 3.5% this time. That was pretty competitive to what was out there for a four year old car. I bought a car that was just a little newer and I'm entitled to discounts on my insurance while I have both vehicles.

I get a multi-car discount on my insurance that between the two cars almost pays the premium on the LeSabre. In addition I got a tax write-off this year for a business use car because it is financed. I allowed one more bank to have access to my checking account. I saved an additional quarter percent off my loan by having my payment automatically deducted from my State Farm checking account. I made sure to set up the due date to be after the fifth of the month so I have enough time to get the money in there each month after my direct deposit.

I do not use my regular checking for my car payment. Instead, I have a second checking account that is strictly for my car payment so I won't mix up my budget. The deposits are simple enough to make since I have the Pocket Agent App on my phone, and I just take a picture of my check. The next day the money is there and four days later, my payment is made. I can completely forget about sending that payment. It also means that because my payment is made automatically each month, I'll never have a late payment so long as I stay on budget and get my deposit in.

By the way, when I went back to State Farm for my financing, I earned another commission on the loan.

I don't think the car you drive defines you. You may look successful if you drive a BMW. I have known several millionaires, and I mean real millionaires that I worked for over the years. They were truly old school and had more money than you could imagine and worked for a company that they could buy and sell over and over again. They drove beaters because they didn't give a second thought what people thought of them. They just go to bed with stacks of money under their mattresses and laugh all the way to the bank while the rest of us struggle to keep up thinking we need fancy wheels to look like we've arrived.

I bought another Buick because my first one was so reliable. It's a 2008 Buick Lucerne. Everyone teases me about driving grandma cars, but then they feel the comfort and see the style of my auto choice when they get in and they shut up.

I looked at the sporty sedans and thought, "How cute!" Cute doesn't fit two adults, three kids and a dog in it to Pennsylvania loaded with presents for the holidays. I also reminded myself that I drive my cars for about five years on average and my girls aren't going to be so tiny forever. I am 5'11" and my daughters are both on their way to surpassing me in height. They wouldn't fit in the back seat comfortably for the next five years so why would I buy something that only suits me for now? I chose something that would suit me now and suit me for as long as it has to! Buy smart.

I have two young children and when I travel out of state, I have lots of stuff to bring. I do not want to drive for three to five hours cramped in a sports sedan with almost no trunk, hitting bumps that make my head hit the roof. I buy based on practicality. The car is stylish and it has far more function and space than I could dream of. It may not sound like I'm telling you anything of value to help you get out of debt, but listen to what I'm saying. Make smarter choices when you do have to make a purchase, especially a big one like a car. If you choose wisely now, you will save a lot more down the road not having to replace it before its time.

I worked for a flavor and fragrance company in Amityville, NY from the time I was 17 until I turned 22. While there I met a man named Stu, who at the time was about 72 years old. This was back sometime in 1993 or so, and I was told he had more money than the president of the company and all the other executives and shareholders combined.

Stu came to work every day in his white uniform shirt and blue uniform pants with his name sewn on the patch of the shirt, just like every other factory worker that was employed there. He drove a 1979 Lincoln Continental that I think he owned since it was new. He maintained the car and that was it. He didn't care what anyone thought of him and he never talked about money. It turns out he was the millionaire next door that no one would have thought twice about. The executives all knew him for years and knew exactly what he was about. They would sometimes pass jokes about how Stu was so tight that he squeaked when he walked. Even as a know-it-all, smart-mouthed 20 year-old, I was enamored of him just for not caring what anyone thought.

These are the tidbits I have learned through my years that I never forgot. They have impacted me more than I even realized because 20 years later, here I am reflecting on them.

I had a job interview in the spring of 2012. There were some unfortunate changes happening in my office that didn't sit well with me, and the writing on the wall told me it might be time to start looking for something else. I happen to excel in my field, so I knew anywhere I did interview, they'd try to get me to sign on with them immediately and bully me if they thought they needed to.

I mentioned earlier one idiot I interviewed with and here comes that story. He was the Vice President of Sales of this up and coming financial services company. As soon as he saw my resume with the production sheet I included, it was on. For someone so savvy at what *he* does, he couldn't hide the ever so slight change in his expression when he saw what I produced in sales each year. I was smart enough to include two years' worth of production on my resume' so it didn't look like one year was a successful fluke.

He tried to woo me into working for him by promising the potential to earn more money than I could ever dream of earning. Everyone says that, but the truth is it is sales. There is no ceiling for income potential if you work super smart and hone your craft. You can make unlimited amounts of money selling anything. I happen believe in the company I work for and I believe in its product. That makes what I do easy because I don't have to force a sale on a client for some product-of-the-month I am peddling. I only sell a product that will benefit the client, and in turn benefit myself. I have to see my clients all the time. Do you think I want to run the other way because I sold them a bill of goods? No. I need to live with a clear conscience.

I've been told I could sell screen doors to a submarine, or ice to the Eskimos.

This guy interviewing me was salivating. He kept me at this interview for much longer than I should have been there. I politely told him several times that I had another appointment to get to and we needed to wrap it up. He assumed I had another interview (which was not the case) and grabbed on with his claws as best as he could. I hate being late but he didn't seem to notice how physically uncomfortable I was becoming sitting there while he went on and on about his success - and how I could have it too. I was shifting in my seat, reminding him that I had another appointment, and my phone was vibrating like crazy in my bag. I didn't dare reach for it, but I knew at that point people were looking for me. This guy just didn't care and I didn't have the balls to get up and walk out. I knew I wasn't taking the job no matter what he offered, but I feared I'd close and lock some proverbial door if I got up and walked out on him.

He then made fun of my car, thinking that it would embarrass me into taking the job. I drove my 2001 light blue Buick LeSabre to his office and parked it right next to his shiny BMW 525i. He must have seen my missing side view mirror (someone had previously stolen my mirror and I wasn't buying a new one).

He taunted me by saying, "You're a single mother driving an old car with a missing mirror and you don't think you need to earn better money?"

I was mortified for a moment and laughed an explanation to him that it had been stolen. It was then that I realized this guy would be the biggest pompous jerk to work for if this is how he talked to me in the interview. Not to mention the fact that he was practically holding me hostage.

I don't need to be shamed into making my life better. The funny thing was, he was trying to hire me! I ran out of that office and thought, maybe he does have a better - no scratch that, not better -*more expensive car*. Then it occurred to me. If he was so successful, wouldn't he be driving the 740iL? Two can play at that judging game.

He got the 5-series because that's all he could swing, and he can probably barely afford the payments while sitting there berating me about my success based on my car. There I was driving a free car! That brings my thoughts back to Stu - the car he drove, and the money he had. For someone who was supposed to be so successful in sales, he gravely misjudged me as a failure based on what car I drive.

How did he know I wasn't sitting on a huge nest egg? Had he been more in tune to his client, he could have invested in his operation big-time! Now when it comes time to figure out where my savings are going to go, do you think I'd go back to him and let him play with my money? Not only did he lose out on a really good hire, he lost out on a potential mega-client. I hope he reads this book and recognizes himself.

I cannot leave out the important fact that I got "caught" going on that interview by my boss. My resume', which was supposed to be distributed tactfully and with extreme discretion, fell into the hands of a friend of his. It was the worst thing that could have happened - at first. Shortly thereafter it became the best thing that could have happened. There was an ugly blow-up between the boss I refer to throughout the book and me. It looked as if this incident was going to be the parting of ways for us but it was not how I intended this to carry out. After some intense, heated, and at times emotional discussions, the lines of communication blew wide open. I was free to express how I felt about our work environment and suggested some helpful adjustments to the office. He seemed to hear me and see it in a whole new light. After careful deliberation and a weekend for me to think about what was put on the table, we both got the tearful happy ending you only see in the movies. I felt appreciated and valued as a team member, and he realized that I never really wanted to leave. Our lines of communication have stayed open since and one of the scariest days I've ever faced, turned out to be one of the best experiences of my career. Ppsssittttooooowwwwwn!!! Uhhhh!

Soup

Habits and being late
Be on Time!

I get up probably a few minutes later than I should in the morning, and I get my girls up and dressed. I make them breakfast, scream, yell, and cry to get them out the door on time so I don't show up even one minute late to work after dropping them at school.

Sometimes I don't know what is better, just being relaxed and a few minutes late, or starting the day stressed and screaming just to be on time. I don't like the feeling of having to apologize to my daughters when they get out of the car for yelling at them to get ready. I don't mind apologizing when I'm wrong, but if I have to apologize it means we've all had a rough start to the day and I hate when I lose it.

In today's day, I can't send them to school without telling them I love them and that I'm sorry for yelling. I don't know if this will be the day they don't make it home from school for any number of God-forsaken reasons. At least they leave with a hug and a FIRM understanding that they are very much loved -even when I yell for them to be on time.

I will always be sure that whenever my children leave my sight, no matter how angry I may be the last words I say are, "I LOVE YOU". I'm also sure not to make my sharing of emotion sound routine, insincere, or muttered like a habit.

That's when no matter how late I may be I stop for ten seconds to look directly into their eyes and explain how much I love them before they leave the car. I will always justify being thirty seconds late for that reason only. I have gone off again on a topic that wasn't originally on my list of chapters to write about but it just came out, so I must have meant for it to be here.

This is not to be misunderstood as a handbook of etiquette or proper behavior because lord knows that some of the stuff that forms in my head and then instantly spews from my mouth would make your head spin and you mother's panties twist.

One of the things I find important for success because it starts the whole range of motion in orbit - is to *be on time*. I'm going to have to strike up a conversation with my boss and give him an apology because unfortunately I'm going to use him as my example shortly.

Everyone is going to be a few minutes late once in a while. That's not what I'm talking about. I'm referring to the people who are perpetually ten to fifteen, dare I say twenty minutes late to everything, leaving others waiting.

These late arrivers might be your co-workers, your date, your friends, or your boss. It doesn't matter. Everyone's time is as valuable as yours and I think people who are habitually tardy are inconsiderate and disrespectful. I'm sorry if you don't like what I have to say, but it all plays into the plan and the bigger picture, and when I'm passionate about something I tend to harp on it…

We need to be responsible for our actions and do what needs to be done in order to succeed in school, and later in life. Being on time is not just for me or for my boss. I'm setting an example for my girls to do the right thing.

I know how much I get wrong all the time, so, I am adamant about the few things I do get right. Their day shouldn't start with the stress of clock-watching from the time they open their eyes until we get in the car, but they are learning organizational skills and proper time management.

I can assure you, I've tried both ways and the stress that accompanies the effort of being on time goes away just a few minutes later and is always worth it.

I'm like a little kid beaming when I walk in the door on time or a little early and my boss sees me. I think, "That's right Boss-man Bing, I'm here, on time, and ready to work." He is able to count on me one more day.

My daughters are learning what it means to be responsible, and know how to appropriately prepare for when people count on them later.

Before I completely beat a dead dog and harp on it anymore, I'll ask you a few simple questions. Is it worth being late? Do you feel rewarded? Does it make you feel good? Do you like to see people disappointed or annoyed? If the answer to those questions is no, then don't do it.

I completely stress if I walk in at 9:01am. No one would say anything to me if I walked in a few minutes late, but that's not the point. My boss relies on me to be there at 9am. That's the starting time. That's the time we agreed on, and I think it makes me look like a better worker if I show up consistently on time. Plus, it makes me feel important. In a simple way it shows I am reliable.

This is the part where I am going to have to sit with him and apologize for using him as an example. My boss is very successful and well liked. In our office we all joke about him being late. I think a lot of it stems from him wanting to get everything done and time just gets away from him. He's pulled in many different directions and always running behind. I joke with people and tell them he'll be late to his own funeral.

After this section, I'm going to have to have a sit-down with him and it'll be like Ricky and Lucy and I'll have some "'splaining to do."

I could have used Daniel as an example of habitual lateness but I've beaten him up enough in this book and I no longer joke about him being late to his own funeral. Who am I kidding? He won't even show up to his funeral. He'll completely forget that he has passed away and won't remember he was supposed to be there.

Daniel is the sweetest man, really he is, and he tries so hard to be on time, he just doesn't know how to manage time. I can see him getting better and he's on the right track. He told me that just the process of me writing this book is already helping him improve. Can you feel me beaming right off the page? I love his indirect compliments. We know each other well enough that we can safely read between the lines and that one made my heart smile.

It reminds me of the scene from "As Good As it Gets" when Jack Nicholson slaps Helen Hunt with that harsh comment about a house dress and then he follows up with, "You make me want to be a better man." Luckily, I got the compliment without the humiliation.

My boss is one of the "late people". He owns the business and doesn't have to answer to me by any means, but it still drives me crazy. He leaves clients waiting. He is late to appointments, has people waiting for him at restaurants, and leaves to go to an appointment that is 20 minutes away two minutes after he was expected to arrive.

It puts me and my co-workers in a bad spot sometimes because we are left to explain to a client that he's running behind when they call. He's not above showing people the respect they deserve. These are our clients - his clients - who we expect to get business from in order to keep our doors open and business thriving.

So let me ask you this, if I'm not even the one waiting for him, and I am irritated that he's making someone else wait, how do you think the client feels when he finally gets there? Will they want that big policy now? Do you think they aren't annoyed because they are going to be late for their next appointment? Now they have less time to discuss what the appointment was about and may not have enough information to make the informed decision of whether our product is the one they want. Add the fact that they feel disrespected, and tell me if you think you're going to improve your business to make more money to pay your bills. That's why we work, isn't it? To pay for the things we want in life?

If you're like me and many other people, you are probably working to pay for the things you already purchased and can't figure out why you're broke. Then you wonder how it got this bad, and what the heck you're working so hard for if you have no money to show for it?

Now that I've thoroughly covered one step in correcting one of many poor choices, get started changing it, and do it on time because it's not too late, yet. Every clock in my house reads the same time and they are all set six minutes fast.

Organize Your Life

Organization is also a huge key to staying on track. I'm going to waiver from using just Daniel and I as examples the whole time because I see examples all around me. I'm going to bring in some friends whom I love dearly, but unfortunately for some of them, they make a great example of what not to do. I want to show you why being on time and being organized helps you keep your money in check.

I'll start on a positive note with my girlfriend Louise. I told her I was putting her in the book and she was flattered.

Louise is a single mother like me, and she separated from her husband a little earlier than I did. That's when we met. I was still married, but our friendship really flourished right about the time I moved out of my house and our daughters were in the same class. Her situation is similar to mine in the sense that we are both smart and savvy with our money and our ex-husbands kind of, well, aren't.

Louise and I make similar salaries but she has a mortgage and pays all of the expenses for her son's hockey. He is not on a regular hockey team. We have a potential Bobby Orr on our hands and he plays in several advanced leagues and travel teams. He is always at practice or playing in a tournament in another state and even Canada. She was just in Boston last week for four days. I thought she was angry with me because I hadn't heard from her. When she laid out what her schedule had been for the week before, I was blown away.

Louise shells out more money for equipment, fees, gas, hotels, tolls, and whatever else this sport is costing her, but she manages to do it without being in debt. Because her son is involved in the types of advanced teams that he is, he can't just play with whatever crappy equipment you can buy at some discount chain. He needs new equipment regularly and it has to be the best because he doesn't just play this sport for fun. I can truly see this kid having a professional hockey career when he gets older and Louise fully supports his ambition, emotionally and financially.

She is at almost every practice, schlepping kids back and forth and balancing her schedule as tightly as I balance my checkbook.

Her credit cards are paid in full every month and she doesn't ever carry a balance if she doesn't have to. There have been times that savvy Louise has carpooled with another mother to share the cost of travelling expenses such as gas, and tolls, so she understands the whole budget thing.

Louise is not someone whom this book was meant for, though I did ask her if she'd read it for me when it was done, to see if she thinks it's worth submitting. She drives an older car that she keeps in good condition like I do, fully paid for and well maintained. We have similar ideals on cars as status symbols and the waste of having unnecessary car payments.

Louise's daughter also participates in the local drama class and soccer. She has practice and plays and opening nights, expensive costumes and equipment too. These activities are costly and I sometimes wonder how she does it, being that she pays for of the majority of the expenses. She still carries her "ex-husband" on her medical insurance.

She bears a huge financial burden all on her own and I pick her brain all the time to see how she does it in comparison to how I do. We talk about money and expenses all the time.

One reason I believe, that Louise manages her money so well, is because she is organized and manages her life well, too. Her home is neat and tidy. Her laundry is done. Her car doesn't have garbage piled up all over in it and she gets her chores done before she goes out for free time or girl time. She won't spend money she doesn't have and understands what sacrifice is.

Did I mention that in her email that explained her schedule to me the other day, she said she had "just downed a PB&J...just another sacrifice." These are her words. She gets it! She is at work making pretty good money and eating a PB&J because she isn't about to waste good money on a paid lunch.

Let's spend a page or two dissecting a few of my other friends, whom I love dearly, really I do. This section is going to sting. Oh am I going to be in hot water after this one! Truthfully this couple would be the last people I'd ever talk about money with or ask advice from. They are such an organizational mess that they don't know which end is up regarding their money, their house, bills, school projects, school closing, or anything else for that matter.

Walk into their house at any given moment and it looks like an actual bomb went off. You can't walk. Laundry is everywhere and I can't imagine how much time, money, and extra detergent are wasted on re-washing clean clothes because you can't tell which pile is which anymore.

The dining room table, well, where is the dining room table? Not kidding. It looks like a shredding factory before the shredding. There is nowhere to sit and eat. They have a state of the art dishwasher but the dishes are stacked in the sink and the stacking has spilled over onto the counter, stove, and everywhere else.

Ask either one of them how it happens, and they both blame the other. No one takes charge or responsibility, and they both live with a defeatist, negative attitude.

She makes a great living but they are so broke because they are the people who buy a new car several times a year. I am not exaggerating, several times a year. I know this as fact and field the phone calls from them regularly when they share with me that they are getting another "car of the season". They have to outdo each other. If he gets a new car, well then screw it. She's getting one, too!

Anytime I have ever walked in their home, they have a new appliance. I mean the *good* ones. I definitely envied their stainless steel French door fridge with the extra drawer for kid's snacks when I first laid eyes on it, but I don't have $2400 for a fridge right now. Besides I'm in an apartment and for now mine is free. I have a cheap laptop that I bought on sale that is equipped with nothing, but it works well enough to write this book. I am even using a free version of Word because I didn't purchase Microsoft Office. It turns out, I found an old Word Document that I emailed myself and just typed over it. Watch out, Microsoft is going to come after me now.

My friends have a new stainless steel dishwasher, but I told you, there are only clean dishes in it that don't get put in the cabinets. A new front load washer and dryer are in the laundry room but no one knows which clothes are clean or dirty.

Their children get whatever they want, whether it is some stupid five dollar toy that disappears in the abyss that is the clutter or a new "pet of the month". There is no fiscal responsibility, nor any other type of responsibility being imparted unto their children.

When the school project is due and it's not complete, it's the teacher's fault for not reminding them. When school is closed for a "professional development" day (whatever the heck that means), it's the school's fault because they didn't get a reminder and she can't find the school calendar amongst the mess.

I have seen piled up food rotting away in their car. I have to take a minute to clarify. I am not trying to bash my friends though I'm sure you'd disagree with that right now. I have a ton of fun with them, and they are great people. I am simply making the comparison of what organization or lack thereof can do to a household and in turn, the finances and the family as a whole.

No one takes the reigns so the bills are paid late or not at all. There is no budget, and the chaos ensues, not allowing them to get out from under the pile they have made. They need to recognize what they need to do, stop whining and blaming the other party, and just do it!

I bet if they tried it for a year instead of taking extra money to have the house painted, they may find that they too can pay their bills instead of filing for bankruptcy…again.

I almost hope they don't read this book because I'll have some more explaining to do. The sad thing is I can easily say I was referring to someone else because I know all too well many families that live like this. It scares me to think that people are professionals with master's degrees who are just so overwhelmed by life they can't get out of their own way to make a bit of difference.

There is someone who I spend the majority of my day with, who is similar to me when it comes to bills and budgeting.

She told me a story the other day about her son who is struggling financially. She had to help bail him out to get his student loan payment in on time. She agreed to wait a week to get the small nominal rent that she collects from him to live in her home. Good for her! He's in his early twenties and should be contributing to the household. The funny thing about her story is that her son asked her to mail out his bills for him. Uh-oh…

Being the mother that she is, and I would have done the same, she saw through the envelope on one of his "payments", and discovered that the reason he was short on his bills was because he was mailing a check to one of his friends for $150 for his fantasy football league.

She was miffed, and I don't blame her. I knew he was going to pay handsomely for that when he got home that day. She's tough like I am and raised her kids on her own without any help from her ex-husband. It goes to prove you can always find money for whatever you want there to be money for.

I allow my children to know about my finances. Maybe not every aspect of them because they are children and there is only so much that they will comprehend but they are part of the budget. I am not going to blindly hand them things in life without them knowing how it came to be or where it came from. They know what it's like to wait for something when there is no money for it this week. I don't scare the crap out of them and tell them that we may not eat next week, but they get the concept of a budget in small ways that will prepare them for being financially responsible when they are adults.

I owe it to them to teach them this. When they ask for something special that isn't on the grocery list, I explain that I've already made the list and there isn't room in the budget for it this week but that I'd happily make room for it next week. They are fine with that. It instills several values in them at once. They understand that they can't have everything they ask for and they understand what waiting for something means. They are also learning that when they grow up, they can do the same thing and avoid the mess I was in.

When I get something on sale and they are with me, I stop and take a minute to explain what I've accomplished. I let them know what it would have cost if I bought it a week prior without waiting. I do the math about how much I saved and offer an example of how I sacrificed something else that I really wanted in order to be able to have that purchase. They get it!

In February 2011 I took my girls to Aruba. By the time we left they understood what $485 for passports meant and what it took for me to get that money. They knew that I took our grocery budget from $150 to $100. We did without an extra side dish at dinner for a month or two to save that money. We ate soup some nights and no one starved.

Their school somehow found so much extra money left in their budget that lunch is free this year for everyone. I still pack my girls a fresh nutritious lunch even though I could save a fortune using that free lunch. My older daughter is a vegetarian and extremely skinny, but naturally so, as is my younger daughter. I must make sure they get the best nutrition because there aren't enough choices for my vegetarian if I use the free lunch option.

With that said, there are days when I have no choice. We'll look at the menu and on pizza day or a day that there is a meatless option for her, I'll let them get school lunch and stretch my groceries for an extra three days. For me stretching my groceries for three days means not having to shop for a week because in three days they are at Daniel's and I don't care what I eat. I don't have to provide anything while they are with him, so if I can wait until next pay period to shop, I've freed up another $100.

My children know this. I explain that we are on austerity and they get a kick out of it because I make it a game. I am not poor and I have the means to provide very well for them, but just because I can afford something doesn't mean they are going to get it. I say, "No" before I say, "Yes" almost every time. I am the queen of maybe, we'll see, I'm not sure yet. They understand disappointment. They understand they don't get everything they want and they understand that I don't work to support their timeframe to get a new bike.

I have very well adjusted girls who really appreciate what they do get. I take them out to dinner now and then but sometimes I deliberately tell them no and make them wait until next week because they appreciate it more and they learn from that. This approach works with adults, too. In fact if *you try* what I'm telling you in this book, you too will earn to wait for things. I'll get to delay of gratification soon.

When I food shop and plan meals, I cook only enough to feed us. That's it. There are not bowls of food in mounds on the table for everyone to just pile on. I know how much my kids can reasonably eat and I make the plates before they hit the table. There is always just a little bit more on the stove in case someone is still hungry, but that's it. If there are any leftovers, it's tomorrow's lunch.

The lesson I teach my children about portion control with food spans across every aspect of our lives. Don't over-eat, over-drink, over-spend. If I raise them to be gluttonous then it'll be my fault when they come to me for a $30,000 loan to save them from foreclosure as adults. It's all relative, the bible tells us so.

I grew up with a skinny mother who could eat all day and night, whenever and whatever she wanted and she just stayed skinny. I know - I want to hit her right now, too. Even now in her sixties, she still looks great. In fact, she's at my apartment right now eating a hunk of Pepperidge Farm Milano Cookie cake. I am not.

My brothers and I didn't get that gene. One brother did, but lost it sometime in his mid-twenties. We ate like horses and there were four of us. I don't know how my mother kept us fed. There were times that she didn't know how she did it either. We were never taught portion control. Any open bag was an empty bag. My mother didn't understand that we weren't built like her and she just didn't see a need to teach us to stop when we had enough.

We all grew up with weight issues and it took me a long time to stop overeating. I still do sometimes, but because it was a lesson that I missed out on, I imbed this into my children every day. Have what you want, but stop when you're full. I teach them to eat healthy and I do my best to focus on nutrition, not weight. Lord knows I don't need them growing up with the eating disorders I faced. It's not that much different with money or any other area of your life - everything in moderation.

Money was different, though. My mother had none and I owe quite a bit of my budgeting skills to her because that woman could take the same nickel that I can stretch into $20 and turn that $20 into food for the week and an electric bill payment.

She was a magician, but word to the wise; do not go ANYWHERE near my mother when she is doing the bills. You'd get the tar beat out of you just for asking what time you had to go to bed if you got her while she was doing the bills, and for the next few days after for that matter. Money was extremely tight or non-existent in our house growing up. There were times that we really didn't know where our next meal would come from.

Heat was absolutely, positively non-existent in our house. I grew up wearing a jacket inside at all times. The thermostat was always pushed as low as it would go which in case you didn't know, is 50 degrees. When we would hear the tick-tick of water running through the pipes on its way to the baseboards because the temperature in house dropped so low that heat came on by itself, my mother would scream, "Hurry! Shut the oil burner off!"

I had no idea that for the twenty-five years that I lived in that house, we were using an emergency shut-off switch on the wall at the top off the basement stairs. I just thought you were supposed to turn the oil burner off when you weren't using it. The rule was, turn it on for ten minutes before your shower then shut it off because there would be plenty of hot water left in the pipes for your shower.

My girls don't have it nearly as bad, but I'd be a fool if I let them know that. They really don't go without, but they appreciate things because I make them wait. In fact, tonight my daughter got so excited about what I made for dinner, that she said, "Oh Mommy, thank you!" I made lamb chops that I bought at a reduced price, steamed broccoli, candied yams, and made us each one garlic knot. I didn't make the whole box of garlic knots because that will go towards another meal and frankly one was enough with everything else I made. My oldest daughter had the same but with vegetarian spare ribs in place of the lamb, just in case you were wondering.

You will not hear my children whine about what I make for dinner. I am not a restaurant and they eat what I give them to eat. They are children and do not rule my house. I rule my house and I am the boss. I waited a long time to grow out of being a child to earn the right to run my household and be the boss. There's not a chance that I'm going to have a smart-mouthed kid putting me in my place. They in turn will earn their way to adulthood at the right speed for which their little minds can handle.

The Sale Begins with the Service

One of my best strengths is my customer service skill. Ask anyone and they'll tell you it's my sales ability. Ahhhhhh, here comes a phrase I'd like to coin. "The sale begins with the service." Try that one on for size. I make it a habit to do right by every client. I am in sales and if I stink at serving the policies I write, my reputation will be for the birds.

I am so good to my clients that most of my new business comes from referrals. I give good service, I get good sales. Just ask Gitomer. I've read his books. I wouldn't dare say that he reminds me of myself but what he has to say in many instances I just completely agree with.

I've had the displeasure of having to help a few clients leave me. That's what I said. I have helped clients take their business elsewhere - temporarily. If they need something that I just can't do for them, like lower their insurance rates, I make sure they are properly protected.

In one instance, I fought as hard as I could to save a sizable household and due to accidents and claims, just could not find another rate reduction or discount for this client that he wasn't already getting. He told me he had no choice but to shop his insurance.

He told me over and over again that he didn't really want to do it. He'd pay more to stay with us, just not as much as he was paying. I understood, but I went further. I asked him to let me help. He was stunned. I explained that he was a valuable client to me and if leaving was in his best interest, it was important that he be properly protected. I didn't want to see him go to some cut-rate insurance company just based on price.

I have a few broker friends in the industry that I would have used for my own insurance if I had not already been an agent. I told my client I'd get him the best coverage for the best price and get back to him. I did just that. I didn't tell my broker friends that they were competing against each other. I just went back to the client with his options and gave him my best recommendation. He is still in awe that I did this for him. I will all but go to the ends of the earth to do what's best for a client even if it's not the best thing for me.

He calls me every few months to see if I can bring him back. He'll pay more to be with me, but I told him I'd keep an eye on the rates and when the time is right, I'll come calling on him. That is service. That is a great habit to have. I hated to see him go and I hated even more to have to tell my boss that we had a client defect because I wasn't able to save it. Rest assured when his children's tickets fall off and the claims have dropped, I will get him a better rate than I ever could. Do you think when I bring him back he will ever leave again after the value I showed him?

Doing the right thing isn't always easy. Sometimes we need to take the blinders off and stop looking at what will benefit us. It's very rewarding to rest my head at night with a clear conscience in the knowledge that I've done right by someone. It's a great habit to get into.

Guess who sends me more referrals than any existing client does? That client does. I reiterate. The sale begins with the service.

Balance Your Checkbook

It's much easier for me to do this now that I'm on my own, but it's another thing doing it when you're not the only adult in the household with a say about where the money goes.

Fees are a means of giving your money away without having anything to show for it. You can always adjust your food budget, or entertaining expenses and incidentals if you put money for those things aside. Next time you don't want to pay your bills on time, tell me and I'll drive by your house so you can throw that extra $35 out the window into the street for me. If you don't want your money, I'll gladly make better use of it than handing it out for foolish reasons such as late fees.

I also avoid ATM withdrawals for purchases because you always have to take out in increments of $20 and you run the risk of having to take out more than you need, leaving the extra cash to burn in your pocket. I debit every purchase unless I'm writing a check. Yes, I am so old school in so many ways that I really do write checks. I will not withdraw money from a foreign ATM. I'd be out of my ever-loving mind if I allowed myself to be charged to access my own money. Foreign ATM's (meaning not your bank, not an ATM in another country), charge you a fee to access your funds through their machine and in most cases, your own bank whacks you with a fee on top of that. I am not going to pay anything, whether it is the one or five dollars it normally totals when you add both fees together, to take my own money out of the bank.

I keep such a tight balance on my checkbook that one day it was off by 0.60 and I couldn't find the error. My math added up. I went back to the previous line in my checkbook register where I had last confirmed the balance and I redid my math. It was still correct.

I went on-line and started matching all of the debits and checks that the bank had cleared to the amounts I had written in my checkbook. I found it! I saw that a check written to my daughters' daycare provider had been cleared for $180.60 and the amount I pay them is always a flat number. I called KeyBank and told them that I wanted my $0.60 back. I knew the tellers at the bank at this point because my office uses that bank for the business account. I sometimes make the daily deposit. The girls at that branch know what a nut I am about my account, and I told them that I would be walking around with a tick until the account balanced again. A few hours later, everything matched up again.

A machine is used to read checks for deposit now instead of hand entering them. Sometimes the machine misreads the amounts because it is reading human handwriting. I looped the zeros on my check in the amount box and the machine picked it up as $180.60 instead of $180.00.

Luckily the discrepancy was only for $0.60, but what if I didn't keep close tabs on my account and that check cleared for $280 instead of $180? I know people that this has happened to and they didn't find out for months because they keep running totals in their head. If that works for you then you're a genius. I don't know anyone who tries to keep a running total of all purchases and debits that doesn't run into insufficient funds fees on a regular basis. The bank didn't pick up on the error, nor did the daycare. If I don't keep track of my own account, I can't expect that anyone else is keeping track. Banks do make mistakes, so I reiterate here, use your checkbook register and track all of your spending. If you only keep track of some of it, then don't bother at all because that's about how effective it will be.

Salad

Free stuff

Don't be afraid to take someone else's throwbacks. After all, they were new once too. When I moved out of the home I shared with Daniel, I took very little furniture with me. I took a small antique sofa that my mother had given me, end tables and a coffee table also from her. Our old kitchen set was out in the garage because it never sold at any of our yard sales. I'm glad it didn't. It's a beautiful table, but I always asked too much knowing its value. I'm so happy to still have that set. I've painted it. Now it looks brand new again and it will last a lifetime. I probably over-priced it subconsciously because I didn't really want to sell it. It was one of the first new items that Daniel and I were able to purchase and it is sentimental to me.

The only new furniture I bought when I moved out was a bunk bed set for my girls with mattresses because they matter more than I do and I wanted something nice for them considering the circumstance. I left the beds they already had at Daniel's and found a furniture store that was going out of business. I scored an awesome set that was originally about $2,000 just for the bunk beds, but I only had $1400 available on my credit card, and I still needed mattresses. It was missing a few slats for the frames. I knew that would be a simple fix and I negotiated hard. I told the salesman who knew he was about to lose a sale, that the most I could afford, hands down, final price, after tax and mattresses included, was $1400 because that's all that I had available on my card. Of course he had to "go talk to his manager" but the store was literally closing its doors in the next few days and they didn't want to get stuck with the inventory. I got them a new bed!

I agreed to take it in "as is" condition, without the replacement slats that were missing and I used scrap slats that work just fine. I took the seats out of the van and made three trips to pick up all the pieces to avoid the $75 delivery charge, but only because the store was close. I'm not about to waste a tank of gas if it'll cost me more to fill it back up than pay for delivery. I made an expensive but necessary purchase and I was smart about it.

The bed has a desk attached and drawers and shelving, so there was no need for any further pieces. I had a dresser from years ago that matched the color. This is still my daughters' furniture and they love it. Every few years they switch who gets the top bunk and everyone is happy.

When we moved into the new apartment, I did not get cable. We lived there for over a year with no TV and no one seemed to notice. The girls played the way kids did when I was growing up. I did pay for internet service because I often work from home and if I was going to make more money I had to spend a few bucks on internet. My heat and hot water were included so all I had to pay was cooking gas and electric. My utilities were minimal. I made do with that little antique two-person sofa and I make do with it to this day.

About eight months ago, a girl at work mentioned that she had a sofa that was practically brand new and that if I wanted it, it was mine for nothing. Her husband even delivered it to me in the back of his truck and I took them to dinner to say thank you. I was starting to fill my living room.

I did take my bedroom furniture because when Daniel and I got married we both had our furniture from when we lived separately. I took mine with me, and he kept his. My mother bought me new dishes at Wal-Mart as a housewarming gift and Daniel and I split the pots and pans. I had a set from my apartment pre-marriage and his aunt had given us a new set as an engagement gift. I left those for him, and took my old set. I left everything else. I did split the silverware and to this day, we are both still using the same silverware.

My point is that you don't have to run out and buy all new stuff because you are starting over. It didn't take me a week to get into this position, and it wasn't going to take me a week to get out of either. You have to have patience. That's why this type of undertaking can be so difficult. You need to learn how to live differently, all over again. You have to remind yourself every day that you're one day closer to your goal. I think so many people give up along the way because it seems like everything is just out of their reach. Remind yourself and do give yourself a pat on the back for every little thing that you do differently and every little accomplishment. If you were going to spend money on something you didn't really need, and stopped yourself, then KUDOS to you! Just don't reward yourself by buying something in its place. That would defeat the purpose, wouldn't it?

I'm in a new apartment now. I moved into my current apartment two years ago because it's nicer and closer to work. The rent is more than the last one but my girls deserved just a little more of the good life. We're in a posh neighborhood and our complex has a pool, tennis courts, basketball court, and a fitness center. My heat and hot water are still included and I only pay electric now. We have central air and when it broke last summer, someone else had to foot the $2700 bill to have it replaced. There are some advantages to renting. Have you ever had to shovel Central NY snow?

I decided to get the very basic cable package because they had an offer for 800 digital stations for about $40 per month. I cannot stop, rewind, or record live television so I actually have to watch a show when it's on or wait for the re-run. Oh poor me. When my introductory rate expires and the price creeps up, even if it's $2 per month, I call them and argue. I tell them to turn it off unless they bring it back down. They will swear up and down that they don't have any other rate to give you, and you need to be prepared to have them call your bluff. As soon as you go through the process of shutting it off and asking where the return center is for the box, a supervisor always steps in and lowers the price.

I traded the internet bill for the cable bill. Some very generous neighbor of mine has unsecured wireless internet and I've been using it for two years. Shhhh, don't tell him. I hope he doesn't ever move out. If I knew where he lived I'd send him a thank you card.

Whenever someone tells me they are getting rid of something, I ask what it is. Let me clarify, I have a beautiful home very tastefully decorated and not filled with the world's garbage I can assure you. I would love new furniture and that will come in time. For now, I live with my floral pattern, Laura

Ashley style sofa and my little antique couch from my mother. I buy accent pieces at Marshall's, Christmas Tree Shops, and Kohl's. Every Christmas I ask for gift cards to any one of these stores where I can go pick something up to make my home fresh and inviting.

I went ice-skating a few weeks ago with my girlfriend Vanessa. It is three dollars to skate and three dollars to rent ice skates. I walked into the locker area where the skate rentals are and struck up a conversation with the kids that work there. It started by them asking what size skate I needed. I just chuckle and tell them I may need a men's size 10 if they don't carry women's size 11 for my giant clod-hoppers. We all laughed about it but before I left for the day, one of the kids told me that a month prior someone left a brand-new pair of men's skates. They were my size and he said I could have them if I wanted them. I walked out with brand-new skates! Don't call me gross for taking someone else's shoes either. I took skates that were worn once or twice by the same person and I no longer have to rent skates that hundreds of people put their stank-nasty feet into all the time.

Vanessa scored herself a pair, too. It turns out some people have so much money that they can just buy new skates and leave their disposable ones behind. The staff said there are amazed at what gets left behind at the ice rink. They hold the stuff for at least a month and if no one comes to claim it, they give it away. Today I was the lucky contestant to win a free pair of new skates.

Pretty soon I am having a free piano delivered. A friend of mine found one on-line and her husband was kind enough to pick it up and will deliver it to me in a few days. I really have some of the kindest friends. I'll make dinner for all of them when they deliver it as thanks. My daughter has the longest fingers and I've always wanted to get her into piano lessons. It's an expense to learn to play and without having one for her to practice on would be an expensive waste.

There is nothing wrong with accepting something from someone at no cost who no longer has a need for it. Things don't have to cost money to be of value, and I will always try to find a way to give back to someone else so the cycle of goodness continues.

Returnables

I take my returnables back. It's the biggest pain in the tucas, really it is, but I can't bear to throw nickels in the garbage. That's what you do if you don't bring them back. You literally throw nickels into the garbage, if you don't return your beer, water, or carbonated beverage bottles. That is the deposit you have to pay in New York State for each bottle when you purchase the beverages. I have an apartment so finding a place to store the empty bottles until I have enough to make it worth returning can be a challenge. Many times I have been food shopping and no matter how hard I try I go about five dollars over budget. That may not sound like a lot to you, but when you keep a budget as tight as I do, five dollars can make or break you. What an adrenaline rush to remember that I brought back $3.65 in returnables offsetting my over-budgeted groceries, returning me to just $1.65 over budget. I can work with that because I can be flexible with my gas money. I over budget on my paper pad by as much as I can so when things like this happen or unexpected expenses come up, I can survive. Sometimes I am lucky and my over budgeting leaves me enough money to take the girls to dinner or put towards a bill.

I have forgotten to use those little bottle return receipts to put towards my purchase more times than I care to admit, just to kick myself in the car when I realize. If I stay on budget, though, I use them as a treat to buy myself lunch one day when I'm hungry. I have taken those little receipts to the grocery store on my lunch break and have been able to buy a big fat apple, two bananas, and small container of sushi. That's a big lunch for me and again I get that little high of walking out with my purchase not having paid anything out of pocket.

When Daniel and I were married, we'd save the returnables in the basement in big black bags for months and it would come out to $20 sometimes. That's half my electric bill now! I have friends and family who refuse to return the deposit bottles so they give them to me. I am not above returning empty bottles.

This doesn't get announced to the world so it's not like I'm walking down the street with a cart going to door to door asking for them, but I just won't throw that money away. I'm not telling you to start collecting bottles to pay your bills. I'm just suggesting that you keep what you've already spent the money on by getting it back from NYS.

I have a vendetta against NYS; I'm not giving them a nickel more than I have to for anything. I know the state brings in huge revenue from what they charge for tolls on the bridges and tunnels, lottery, taxes, and everything else. When the state says they have no money and I have to wait to get my tax refund, I make the decision to get every penny I'm owed from them.

Sorbet - the palette cleanser

Know your prices

Know your prices. This is so important that I can't stress it enough. I am no longer embarrassed or afraid to speak up when my total doesn't match what I estimate it to be. Add up what you're spending as you go or at least stop for a minute before you get to the register to do quick math to see where you are. I don't calculate the tax ahead of time at the grocery store, but I do everywhere else. If it's a dollar or two, I don't usually say anything but I double check the receipt after I get off the line to be sure. The reason I don't calculate tax for the grocery bill is because there are usually very few items that get charged tax, but for clothes and any other purchase, you do get taxed. If you don't include this in your total, you can go over budget and by quite a bit if it's a big purchase.

Know your total means if you've added up what you spent, and it should come to around $25-26 and the cashier asks for $32 then something is wrong. You should speak up. It's your money, why would you just walk away?

It happened to me a month ago at the grocery store. I was in a store that I don't usually food shop in but I knew that one item on my list was on sale for half of what it would cost me normally. I do not think that you should drive to five stores to save five cents because that's a waste of time and gas, but I was already in that shopping center. When I got inside for the one item, I found some other great deals that really surprised me. It wasn't near payday yet but I had $32 left in my checking account and knew that whatever I bought would come off of the next week's grocery list. If I could save a few dollars I would.

I knew exactly what my total should be when I got to the register. It was supposed to be $28. The cashier told me the total was $36. I said, "No, something's not right." She looked annoyed and a little nervous because I told her that I added everything up before I got there and it should be $28. I didn't know this store too well and couldn't figure out what the heck her register was doing as far as adding and subtracting the discounts. You need to be a rocket scientist to understand some of these receipts and I swear they do it deliberately to confuse consumer. I bought a bunch of soup that was buy one get one free. Apparently, the register rings it all up at regular price then takes it off at the end. I went through my stuff (there wasn't that much) right in front of her and said, "Look, this costs this, and that costs that. How do you explain why it came back so much higher?"

A manager finally came over, and by now too much effort had been put in for me to walk away, and sure enough it didn't make sense to the manager either. Two of my soups rang up regular price, not giving me one for free, which in turn caused another soup to ring up differently because it didn't look like I bought the right quantity to get the sale. They were $2.69 each, and I was charged for three of them instead of one. The other item was my Fiber One bars. They were 3 for $6, and that's a huge steal so I bought nine boxes. They should have cost $18 but two of the boxes rang up $3.69 each and in the end I almost paid $12 more all while potentially overdrawing my account.

Remember, I was spending $28 and I only had $32 left in my checking. If I paid $36 because I didn't want to haggle over the correct price, and if I didn't know my bank balance, I would have overpaid by $8 and been charged a $34 overdraft fee. That little mistake could have turned into a $42 nightmare over $28 worth of groceries. That could have caused a snowball effect of money lost in my checking account. If I were charged an overdraft fee, I would have to make that up in addition to the extra amount I was charged on my groceries. The situation would have required therapy if my checkbook were off. We're talking padded cell kind of stuff. If I get charged a fee for screwing up my checkbook, I take it personally because I work so hard to keep it straight. I'm not going to let some cash register send me to the nuthouse. I'll send myself there; I don't need any help thank you very much. Not on my 6-minute-fast watch!

Another example is JC Penney's. After my youngest daughter's birthday party in January, (I had to give her a party because I gave one to my other daughter last summer) one of my girlfriends decided to stop at JCPenney after I told her about the awesome deals I had witnessed the week before.

Daniel and the girls got me the most beautiful workout outfit for Christmas. The girls helped pick it out and although I was totally flattered, I couldn't get the top on…at all. Now, I have the world's smallest boobs. I'm not just a member but I am the president of that club, so why the heck couldn't I get this top on?

They had accidentally bought me an x-small. It was a sweet gesture, but I am a size small. When I went to exchange it, I saw what Daniel had the gall to spend on it. It seemed every other workout top was on sale or clearance, but not the one Daniel bought. I exchanged that one top for five tops, one pair of workout pants and a sports bra. I even got a dollar back! I hurt Daniel's feelings, though. He knew I needed to exchange the size, but when I told him what I wound up with, he was pretty miffed. He told me he had picked something for me that cost so much more because he wanted me to have something nice. He knew I would never spend the money on myself, and because it was Christmas, he wanted to splurge. He knows I buy some of the cheapest crap for myself so I can use that money to buy the girls better stuff and I had ruined his gift to me. Once in a while it isn't worth saving a few bucks, and I felt really bad. It's ok, though. Daniel was ticked off enough that he went off on me so badly, it turned my guilt into anger and I called him a jerk among other things.

My point of this story is that on my way out, I noticed the children's section had a ton of stuff that was between $2-5. The girls didn't actually need clothes but they could use a few things that were getting worn and truthfully half of the stuff I buy them winds up at Daniel's and I never see it again.

I went back to JC Penney's a week later with my girlfriend. I had gotten paid and we pretty much cleaned out the kids' department. She didn't buy as much as I did, but we couldn't help ourselves.

The stuff had been marked down even further than the week before. I got summer clothes ahead of time, clothes to start them off for school next year, pajamas, and a ton of stuff to wear from now until that in-between time where spring is on its way, but not really warm yet.

When it comes to my girls I do tend to splurge a little more but not too foolishly. There still has to be a need or something close to it. I had so much stuff that the sales people were taking things off my arms to bring to the register. Although it's a great gesture and it gives my tired arms a break, it throws me off because I keep adding up my total as I buy. When I was done I went up to the register and told her to help the next person because I needed a minute to assess what I had and see where I was.

I did my quick math and totaled that 65 items should come to $206. I don't ever open new accounts to save 10% just to give it back in interest, but today they were offering 20%. I mentally agreed that I would pay it off in one shot interest-free. I figured that at $206 I would save a little more than $40, so it would mean I just bought clothes for two growing girls for a period of over three seasons for a total of $160 and that made it worth it.

I applied for the account with my fingers crossed not fully knowing if I'd be approved but low and behold I was! My total was $320 *before* the 20% was taken off. I stopped in my tracks and said no way Jose! I insisted it should not have been more than $206 before my discount. They had to open another register and re-ring everything one at a time. Due to new markdowns some items marked $2 were ringing in at the original $28 price. Guess what the new total was after they corrected their prices? It was $206 before my 20% discount.

My total was $162 before tax and I think spending the ten minutes that it took to re-ring everything was well worth my $114 dollars. It was like getting paid $114 for ten minutes worth of work. So I say again, know your prices and don't be afraid to question things when they don't add up right.

My girlfriend stood there in awe. She couldn't believe how bad the discrepancy was. I'm not saying anything negative about Penney's because the salesgirl told me that they had just marked more stuff down that morning and the computers just didn't tally it correctly. She was very nice and extremely helpful. My friend was now standing there with *her* bags in hand wondering if she had just paid too much but was still too uncomfortable to ask! I flat-out said to her in front of everyone, "Just look at your receipt. If it's correct, we'll leave. If it's not, just have it adjusted."

Why would she want to give her money away? It made no sense. The sales girl confirmed that she made sure her purchase rang up correctly so she should be all set, and my friend accepted that!

Think about this, she bought her stuff *before* me, so how could the cashier have known there were price discrepancies until I made her aware of them? We bought some of the same stuff. After seeing what happened to me, would you have walked out without at least reviewing your receipt?

I am going to search for my favorite Kohl's receipt. I hope I still have it. I'll be so upset with myself it I don't have because this receipt is worthy of being framed and hung in the Smithsonian.

When I shop at Kohl's and on more than one occasion, I have had people watching what I do and because I'm so energetic and fun, I wind up yelling the store's slogan, "The more you shop, the more you Kohl's!" before I leave. I have amazed people at what I can do during a sale with a coupon, good math, the patience to wait to shop on the right day, and of course, Kohl's cash.

During the holidays, Daniel and my friend Josh wanted to utilize the awesome 30% off coupon I had but they didn't have a Kohl's card. They asked if they could make the purchase on my card to get the savings. I only did it for one reason, well two actually.

The first reason I would allow someone to use my card is because they agreed to have the purchase rung up and totaled after the discounts then have the order suspended. Once the order is suspended, they in turn make the exact payment of what they were buying on my card so I would not be getting stuck with someone else's purchase, nor would I be paying interest if they paid to me at a later date.

The second reason is because those purchases earned Kohl's Cash and if you think for a second that I'm fessing up that Kohl's cash to them after I gave them the convenience of saving 30% by using my card you are sadly mistaken. I did them a solid. They can let me have the Kohl's cash. They had each accumulated about $20-30 and really wouldn't be back to use it before it expired and I had about $40 of my own to add to it.

My daughter needed a new winter coat. You could almost see her elbows because the sleeves on her old one were getting too short. I bought $155 Zero Xposure, four-in-one jacket system for our winters here, and I bought it two sizes too big. It fits her with plenty of room and by golly she will definitely get two winters out of it. Three if I can push the envelope. I also had a ton of other stuff that totaled almost $300.

There was a couple on the line in front of me using Kohl's cash and when they were done, the cashier told them they still had $3.96 left to use. They told the cashier to save it for someone else because they wouldn't be back before it expired. I immediately piped up and said, "Can I be the lucky contestant to have that Kohl's cash?" They laughed and said, "Yes." With their Kohl's cash added to mine I had $93.96 to spend.

The jacket was on hold because the pretty purple one that my daughter liked was in limited quantity now that it was on clearance. I didn't want to buy it before the Kohl's cash was eligible for use in three days. I grabbed that coat at 55% off, and put it on hold. When I came back, it was 60% off. Woo Hoo! I got extra Kohl's cash from the people on line in front of me. I also received another coupon in the mail that started that day.

After the sale, the coupon that gave me an additional 20% off, and my Kohl's cash, I paid $0.53 out of pocket. Yes, I said I paid *fifty-three cents*! If I can find the receipt I will put it in this book so you can see it for yourself. The woman on line behind me went crazy asking how I just pulled that off. I told her how and she said she was going to start shopping there more now that she understood how it worked. I heard her still talking about it as I was exiting the store, and that's when I yelled back, "The more you shop, the more you Kohl's!" There should have been a camera crew on-hand because that was a commercial if I'd ever seen one.

All of these little things I do are ways to save money. Then take what you save and apply it to bills that you don't want to have to pay forever.

I also return bad food. I pay good money for my food and sometimes I have to wait to buy the things I want or need. Imagine my disappointment when I finally get everything I need and two days later it is spoiled because it was left out at the store or I got someone's check-out reject. Remember my daughter is a vegetarian and I stock lots of fresh fruits and veggies for her. I am not going to pay $6 for a special cheese for her to have it turn blue in a few days when the date tells me I have two months. I take it right back and get a new one.

Dinner Conversation

There's money for everything

I'm going to tell you a dirty little secret about me in a minute because I have an expression that I use. It's officially my quote because I'm putting it in my book. So now I own it. Here it comes… *"There is money for whatever you want there to be money for"*.

I mean this in a realistic sense. I'm not saying there is money to buy a yacht. I'm saying that if you wanted to, you could come up with money for things you didn't think you could if there was reason enough to. Just ask an out-of-work smoker. No matter how late the cable bill is or whether the lights are going to get shut off, if you want something badly enough, you will find a way to get it and pay for it. A smoker absolutely has to buy cigarettes. Now don't misunderstand me, I'm not knocking smokers.

I know this to be a fact because I smoke. That's right. I waste so much of my hard-earned money on the worst, most expensive habit in the world and no matter how tight my budget is there was always room for a pack of butts - because I make sure there is. I'll skip new shoes for a year or not buy any new clothes to make room for that… because I want it, or need it - I can't really tell anymore.

My point is, if you can force yourself to have the discipline to find a way to come up with almost $10 per day for your butts (that's what they cost where I live), then you can find a way to stay on a budget and get your debt paid off. Don't argue with me either by saying that you buy the cheap generic ones, or go the reservation to buy them. Whatever! You get the point. They're still really expensive.

My point again is "there is always money for whatever you want there to be money for." So you say you don't smoke. Please don't tell me you me you can't find somewhere in your budget, money that you waste - excuse me spend - on items that you could skip but don't want to so you justify paying for them. Let me into your house and I'll show you where it can come from. Is it coffee? Some people will pay $5 for a cup of coffee and sometimes do that several times a day, but then they don't understand my vice for smoking – I say we're even. I have been in line behind people who are buying groceries with a Benefit card, and paying cash for $60 worth of lotto tickets. Here's the winning ticket: put that money in a good interest bearing account or invest it in life insurance which is sure to get you a bigger return right now. You'd have much more money than if you kept thinking you were going to buy the winning ticket.

Maybe you buy lunch every day, or even a couple times a week. Stop, or at least cut back. It'll save you, I swear. For every two, four, or eight dollars I calculate I save by not spending adds up to $35 or more by the end of a week or two. This is about how much my electric bill is. Done. Bill paid. Buy Starbuck's in the bag, and brew it at home. It's still expensive, but it's cheaper than paying them to make it and while you sacrifice the luxury of walking in and ordering it, you can still enjoy it and save money. Compromise.

If I called you tonight and said I have a free trip to the destination of your choice, hotel and airfare paid, and all you had to do was come up with meals and spending money, you'd find a way to do it because you WANT TO. You'd be the savviest shopper and budget-keeper all week if I told you that you had a week or two to come up with the money for the trip. Suddenly you'd realize that you could do without a lot of the stuff that you spend money on because the reward of the trip seems worth it. Well, why not do it for yourself? The reward for getting out of debt is well worth it, I assure you.

You have to want to be out of debt badly enough that you are willing to sacrifice everyday gratifications over and over again for the benefit of what the end result will do for you. It will free up so much money to buy things you really want. I was paying over $500 per month in credit card bills until they were paid off, sometimes more when I could. I was making as big of a payment as I could, literally leaving myself with nothing, and I mean *nothing*.

On any given day, my checkbook could go as low as $0.38. Now that those bills are gone, I am banking that money for something I really want.

I write every single transaction into my checkbook before I walk away from the register. I repeat, I write EVERY transaction into that little blue checkbook before I leave the store. I know what it is in there *to the penny* every minute of every day. I have to if I am going to leave myself practically nothing until the next pay period. I cannot run the risk of getting hit with an overdraft fee. Do not think that you can accurately keep a running total of your bank balance in your head, along with all of your transactions. If you can, and you've never gotten an overdraft fee, then you're a genius and I'd like to meet you. I hear people tell me this all the time. It is not possible. The same people who tell me that they do this are the same people begging me to return their overdraft fees because they bounced their insurance payment, again.

I've discussed the subject of smoking several times in this book. Louise was a smoker when we met but quit shortly after. I don't even recall what she looks like with a cigarette, and I applaud and commend her on her tenacity. I know how much goes out the door each month on my habit, and even though I can see what it adds up to, I was blinded-sided by a little tidbit that Louise shared with me.

We both live similar lifestyles and share the same habits. We are both in the same boat as far as having any real savings…or so I thought. We were discussing money and finances again as we normally tend to do, and she confided in me that she recently leant her ex-husband a generous sum of money to help him out of a bind.

When she told me that he asked her for $3600 and that she had it on-hand to loan him, I was floored. I had to temporarily put aside my desire to shake her for being willing to fess up such a chunk of greenage when she wasn't sure he how was going to be able to reimburse it. I flat-out asked her, "Louise, you had $3600 just sitting around available to loan him? I thought you and I both pretty much depleted our savings to keep our expenses and budgets in the black."

Louise was so cool with her response. She said she didn't want to sound as if she was getting on her high horse or like one of those "reformed smokers". Over time she started putting what she was spending on cigarettes into an account and before she knew it, she had that much, and then some.

You can imagine how much more of an impact that had on me than previously. You see, there are levels of what people need to see to be fully impacted by what a change can do. People who buy cigarettes one pack at a time and don't see the money disappearing might be moved to see in my budget where I allocate $300 per month for them. I got used to seeing the $300 disappearing from my budget and was dulled by the thought of saving that money, but hearing the chunk that I was giving away in one-lump sum like $3600 became very tempting.

Louise went on to share that it wasn't just the cigarettes. It was the other items she would grab that were impulse purchases when she ran into the store for her daily pack. I agree with that statement because I spend a lot of money on gum. Granted I want fresh breath anyway, but I buy and chew more gum than most people, in order to avoid smelling like a tobacco factory when I'm talking to people.

Louise saved $3,600! That is what I would save in one year if I quit. I am debating if that is going to be my next big challenge or not. I know I need to do it, but I believe in setting realistic goals that I will succeed at. Although I know it is an excuse, I will not succeed right now. I am not ready but when I am, I will follow my own advice, quit and put that money to greater things in my life. Maybe I'll buy myself a pair of tastefully sized boobs.

For now, I'll live by my own words that there is money for whatever I want there to be money for. I give to various charitable organizations when I can and when I am so moved to. I give to my church, the animals and sick children. The rest of you can fend for yourselves! If you are able-bodied and not helpless then help yourself – and then help others.

It brings me to the point of the old saying "one good turns deserves another". Every time I help someone or give to someone in need, I find I truly am paid back ten-fold in many different ways. If you're going to try this, clear your conscience and be sure that your heart and your intentions are pure or don't try at all. If you give openly and sincerely, God or the Universe, or whatever you believe in, will be sure to provide for you. In my case, God has never let me down. I get exactly what I need. On the rare occasion that I wonder why I don't have more, in reflection I get the answer that I'd completely screw it up if I had more. I am again happy and appreciative of what I have in the knowledge that I have all I need. What a mess the world would be if we all won the lottery simultaneously. Talk about utter chaos.

I sacrificed for a long time and now I have earned some good, flavored coffee. Keep in mind that this did not become a free-for-all. I still buy store brand, but my local grocery store Wegmans, offers some really good gourmet coffee for a lot less than the competitors. They also have bulk bins that let me choose how much I want to buy. That allows me to buy more or less to keep the grocery list on budget like I do with fruits and veggies. I supplement that coffee with another cheaper plain coffee. If the flavor is strong enough, I will mix the flavored coffee with the plain coffee so I can enjoy more of it at a lower cost. Sometimes I think if I don't moisturize enough, I may start to squeak like Stu.

I have found money in my budget for better coffee because I wanted to. *There is money for whatever I want there to be money for.* This week, I want there to be money for a better cup of coffee!

There is also money for life insurance. My monthly insurance bill is $414.85. You might think I have expensive car insurance. The portion that is for car insurance is about $110 for two cars with full coverage. The rest goes to life insurance.

You read that correctly. I spend almost $300 per month on life insurance. The method to my madness is that I have no spare money to give my girls for a wedding, to start a business, or to buy a house. They have college funds, but I don't have extra money to hand them a chunk to give them that shot in the arm in life. Several of my friends' parents and relatives of mine like aunts and uncles had the money to pay for my friends' and cousins' educations or house down payments. I didn't have that growing up. Although I don't plan on just forking over a large sum of money to my girls, I want to have something in place for them and I have chosen life insurance.

You know by now that I am an insurance agent and I know full well what these policies can do for them later in life, whether it's my $550,000 death benefit *to* them or the policies I put in place *on* them. The policies are earning guaranteed cash value for them when they become adults. There is no guarantee in the stock market. Maybe they'll never have to touch the cash value. I hope they don't have to, but it'll be there for them just in case.

I don't want to get morbid or touch on the subject of what kind of catatonic state I would be in in the event of the loss of one of my children, but unfortunately it happens. I didn't buy it for that reason, but heaven forbid I am ever in that position, you'd find me rocking in the corner sucking my thumb for an ungodly amount of time and I would still have to provide for my other child. It is also there for that. I won't be heading back to work or reality and I'm not even going to be able to function on my own for quite some time. In that case, I have it for that, too. I can stay home and grieve.

I have the best policies I could buy for their long-expected futures. I put riders on these policies that grow the death benefit. By the time my girls are married and having children of their own, they may not ever have a need to purchase more life insurance. It will be locked in at the price for a three-year old because that's how old they were when I started buying it.

Not everyone has to get as much life insurance as I have. The $300 I spend is not for one policy. That money pays for seven different policies that I have acquired over time. I have added to it as I was able to afford to and here is a breakdown of what I have, what it costs, and the benefit of what each policy offers my girls and me.

Be patient because at first I'm just going to put out what I have and what it costs. Afterwards, I'll breakdown what it all means so you can understand.

- Heather, $250,000, 20-year term, $24 per month.
- Heather, $250,000, 20-year return of premium term, $44 per month.
- Heather, $50,000 15-pay life, permanent insurance, $101 per month.
- First daughter, $25,000 Whole Life with riders for GIO and WPD, $18.62 per month.
- Second daughter, $25,000 Whole Life with riders for GIO and WPD, $18.62 per month.
- First daughter, $25,000 Universal Life, Option 2, death benefit increasing, riders for GIO and WPD, $26 per month.
- Second daughter, $25,000 Universal Life, Option 2, death benefit increasing, riders for GIO and WPD, $25 per month.

The first policy is a term policy and only offers coverage for the twenty years that I locked the rate in. At that point, it can cease or I can renew at the rate that will be charged at the current age I am at renewal which in my case will be 53. This type of policy offers great coverage for a nominal price and in twenty years I won't need as much because my children will be grown. I won't need to protect their future like I do now. I am covered until age 53.

My return of premium policy is also term but with a twist. It costs more than the traditional term policy but if no benefit is paid, meaning I haven't kicked the bucket, then I get it all back. This is a small investment at $44 per month. I get the same great coverage but if I am still alive at the end of the twenty years, I get every penny back tax-free because it is paid for with net dollars and doesn't earn interest. This means it is not a taxable event. Again, in twenty years my children will be grown and I won't have a need for that much coverage anymore. I am covered until age 54 with this policy and this gives me a supplement to retirement. I will have paid a total $10,560 and while my girls will get $250,000 if I die, I receive a check for $10,560 before I retire to use however I want. Maybe I choose to pay off a mortgage or invest in my savings, or just put it somewhere to live off of. The possibilities are endless.

A Fifteen-Pay Life is a permanent policy that never goes away (unless I die of course) or I cash it in. The policy is locked in for the rest of my life but the payments are condensed into fifteen years at $101 per month. I stop paying on it after fifteen years, yet it continues to grow dividends and cash value until I either die or cash it out for a whopping sum of money. The illustration for my particular policy shows that at age 62, I will have $35,557 in available cash value to use towards retirement, cash out, or just leave there to keep growing. The death benefit will have also grown from its existing $50,000 to $77,082. By the way, as this policy grows cash value I am afforded the option of borrowing against it if I needed to. I don't recommend doing this unless you have to, but in many cases the interest on a life insurance loan is much lower than a traditional loan.

I put this policy in place because I won't have the term insurance anymore by that time and I still want to make sure my family doesn't get stuck burying me in a pine box in the backyard. I am not going to burden them with my final expenses, plus it will be a nice little check they get by the time the death benefit grows. That policy will start increasing in death benefit over the years. I opted for paid up additions instead of receiving the dividend check each year from what it earns so it buys it more insurance.

My daughters both have $25,000 whole life policies that I purchased when I was a brand new agent. I didn't know the ins and outs of insurance but was eager to start selling and earning commission. I did so by purchasing these policies. Whole life is also a permanent policy and a great one at that, but as I grew as an agent, I learned about the benefits of Universal Life.

Whole life locks the rate in for the age of the insured when the policy is purchased. It will earn cash value and dividends much life the 15-pay but you can't change it unless you are exercising the GIO rider. GIO means guaranteed insurability option. At certain intervals in my daughter's life, the insurance company, and in this case State Farm, offers the right to exercise that option. It allows me to purchase additional insurance without having to show insurability. It's great if you're sick, have medical ailments, etc., because you can't be turned down. I've paid a few extra dollars a month for this rider and I recommend it to everyone. There are so many diseases out there today and with how scary it can be, there really is no telling if my children will wind up with diabetes or God-forbid something worse.

When they are adults getting married and having children they can increase their coverage when they need to. I've made sure they will not have to go through the physicals, interviews, and medical underwriting associated with life insurance by putting this rider on there for them.

I've also included WPD that means waiver of premium for disability. I can sign ownership of these policies over to them at age 21 or whenever I think they are mature enough to handle the responsibility of paying the premiums. This rider will pay the premium on the policies if they ever become disabled for a length of time. If they can't afford the premium due to limited income from disability, the policy won't lapse and they won't call their agents to cancel the policy when they think they can't afford it. The premium does not need to be paid back if they are no longer disabled, either.

Once I started learning more about the options that were available with different life policies, I discovered the beauty of Universal Life. Universal

Life is flexible and can be changed to adjust the premium or the death benefit if need be. There are two options, Option 1 death benefit level, and Option 2, death benefit increasing. Option 2 costs more, but I bought it when they were six and eight years old so I pay about $25 per month each.

This policy grows the death benefit while paying a guaranteed amount of interest throughout the life of the policy. It may perform better depending on market conditions, but I locked them into a guaranteed interest rate of 4% meaning if the market plunges, the policy will never drop below 4% interest. Try getting that kind of guarantee from a bank or an investment.

When I said my children might never need to purchase more insurance it is because this policy will have an increased death benefit every year and by the time they are adults with a true need for life insurance it will no longer be a $25,000 policy. The death benefit will have grown immensely and will more closely fit their need than just having a little life policy that Mommy started when they were babies.

I don't want to get too detailed here about the life insurance because this is not a sales book for insurance. I just want to give you the basics of why I chose to put these plans in place. If anyone really has a need more information, talk to your local insurance agent or feel free to contact me. I'd be happy to give you a more detailed explanation. Keep in mind I am only licensed in NY and rules are governed by state.

I'm telling you all of this because I want you to see what I have put into place even when times were tough and I thought I had no money for such a plan. I have said before, if I can afford to buy cigarettes, at about $300 per month then I certainly can come up with at least as much to protect my family and secure their future. I've come to expect this is what my insurance premium is every month just like my rent and I don't see it as discretionary income. For me, this is a necessity and I have the means to provide it.

I did not run out and purchase all of this in one shot, either. I purchased each policy when I could afford to and added to them over time. There is a four-year span over which the purchase of these policies is spread. I also make a commission from each policy so I wasn't completely fool-hearty when I decided to buy.

Daniel I started out with the inexpensive term policies because it gave us the coverage we needed at a price we could afford at the time. Next I bought the juvenile Whole Life policies for the girls. After I started getting established and earning better commission, and after I was used to paying the existing premiums, I added the 15-pay.

Return of Premium term wasn't even available at first but as soon as I heard we were offering it, I jumped on it. It offers the best of both worlds. This policy is the answer to every financial planner who tells you to buy term and invest the rest. You're getting a term policy relatively cheap - much cheaper than permanent life - but you're not just giving your money away because you get it all back. No one benefits from a term policy except the beneficiary. It still serves its purpose to cost-effectively protect your family. Return of premium and permanent insurance offer living benefits, too and since I don't have a 401K, it performs double duty by acting as a cushion for my retirement.

Return of premium is like leasing an apartment for twenty or thirty years, paying your rent and getting your protection. At the end of lease, imagine your landlord handing you a check and saying, "Here is every penny back you've ever paid in rent. Thank you for allowing me to invest it while protecting you." That is how I describe it to my clients so they understand it. I've just sold it to myself right here in the book, so why wouldn't I have it?

I'm not trying to make this a handbook about insurance sales. I'm just showing you where I choose to find money in my budget to plan for my future and my children's future. There is no doubt, no way around it. I am going to die and so are you.

If I die before my time, my girls will receive $250,000 each and my ex-husband will receive $50,000 to help offset the cost of raising them alone. Why? Because I care. Why? Because I can.

I tell people all the time that don't think they need life insurance that they can just call me fifteen minutes before they die and as long as they're still eligible, I'd be happy to put that policy in place for them.

Guess what I tell people who sit in front of me - their little child plays with the bead table in my office - and say they just can't afford it right now? I tell them that there is money for whatever they want there to be money for.

Entrée

The budget

After I got that sweet little shot in the arm from Daniel's 401K split, I paid the smallest balance first. Then I took what I would have used for those payments and added it to the payments I was making on other bills so I could tackle them faster. I also closed every unnecessary account so I would never have to think about them again. Besides, what would I need with a Home Depot card if I no longer owned a home?

I only kept two major credit cards open. One is my State Farm Visa because it only has a manageable $1,000 limit. I can't get myself into too much trouble with that. The other is my Capital One Visa because it has a $3500 limit. I wanted that just in case I ever faced an emergency that I didn't have the cash on hand pay for. I also still owed a ton of that card and didn't want to close it with a balance. I am extremely careful not to use that card unless I have to. It's very easy to get used to looking at a small $300 balance, watch it creep up to $800, get used to seeing that, and then allow it to get to $2400 before you know it. I have done that. I told you I'd tell you the mistakes I've made, too. That feeling stinks, but it's like ruining a diet. Eat too much on one day and if you don't get back on the wagon fast, you'll gain back more than the ten pounds you lost to begin with.

I developed my budget using a simple 5X9 Safelite Auto Glass pad that I have grown to love and depend on so much that I can't use any other. When I run low on them, I call my rep and request he bring me more. I don't use a fancy spreadsheet or software program. I simply use a pad and I list every single item that I can foresee having to spend from each paycheck. I get paid twice a month, on the fifth and the twentieth.

It took some getting used to, but I know all of the due dates on my bills, and which check each bill needs to be paid from. At the top of the page, I write the pay date. Underneath that I start listing all the bills that are due. I don't start filling in the amounts until after I am sure I haven't forgotten any. I don't want to have to go back to make messy adjustments. Once I have everything listed that is due before the twentieth, I start adding in the column with the amounts of the bills that are the same each month. I enter rent, insurance, groceries, cable, gas, cigarettes, and the automatic payment that comes out for one credit card. Because I work in sales, the paycheck that comes in on the fifth always varies because it includes my base salary plus the commission I've earned from the month prior.

Don't ever let anyone tell you that being in sales is easy. It can be very difficult to get your bills covered if you have a bad month, or several, but it can also be very lucrative. Based on what I've produced the month before, I can estimate what my direct deposit will be.

I say estimate because I get hit with a ton of extra taxes from the first check of each month. This is because the IRS calculates taxes based on the number of pay periods and I have twenty-four of them being that I get paid bi-monthly. If you take that first check (that I really only get twelve times per year) and multiply it by twenty-four pay periods, it appears that I make much more money than I actually do. This bumps me up to the next tax bracket. I get whacked at the 33.5% rate on most of those checks and more recently it has risen to 34.75%!

On the top right side of the page I enter the amount next the word "in". I then add up the total of the expenses that don't change, and see how to best allocate the rest of what is left on the remaining bills. Once I have all of my numbers, I put the amount of what I will send out under my income next to the word "out". I usually only leave myself an extra $20 if it's even available for some flexibility. On a good month, I can send quite a bit more money towards the balances that I am trying to pay off, with the largest chunk going to the card with the smallest balance. When that one is paid in full, I again add that payment to the other cards and attack them next. It's called divide and conquer.

Don't take that money and spend it on anything else. In a less productive pay period, I barely cover everything. That's when it gets really tight and adjustments to groceries and gas are made. I can only do this because I try to over-budget, just slightly wherever I can so if I need a tiny reserve, it is available for me. I don't necessarily use $150 worth of gas each pay-period, though sometimes I do depending on the price of gas. When I don't, it's reallocated or saved for the next pay period when I may be a little short. If I have used my budget and I'm not getting paid soon enough, I can gauge how long my gas will last, and I kid you not, I will not drive anywhere unless I absolutely have to. This is where the extreme discipline comes into play. I have to live this way if I want to reach my goal. I was not playing around when I told you that although the concept is easy, the action to stick with it is not!

The next pay period consists of just base salary and is a very different paycheck indeed. This is what is used for the smaller remaining monthly bills, but still includes the regulars like gas, groceries, cigarettes, etc. I repeat the same thing with my pay pad, but I also start on next month's sheet. I know which bills are due every month and by the twentieth can gauge what the next check on the fifth will look like. My pay pad is always filled out a month to a month and a half in advance. I use the previous month as reference to be sure I haven't forgotten anything. I do not discard the sheet from the last deposit until the next deposit so I can double-check and recalculate that every penny is accounted for.

The first thing I do every single morning when I get to work is balance my checkbook against my on-line account. I have it down to such a science that it can be done in less than two minutes. That is also true because I do it every day and there is very little updating to do to keep it current. I make sure that my balance matches theirs. If it doesn't, I do not let it go until I find out why. I write every purchase in my checkbook and I put a check mark in the column where you mark that it has cleared or is pending. All pending transactions get a check mark, and when it is officially posted, I write the date that it cleared under the check mark. At least twice on every half page of the register, I put a line all the way across the page after I have balanced it, and include the date on the line. If ever my numbers don't match the bank's numbers I only have to go back as far as the previous line to find the discrepancy. I cannot stress to you enough how important it is to know exactly how much money you have in your account. If you keep your records current, you cannot incur unnecessary fees and charges by miscalculating how much you thought was there - and you'll know how much you have available when you need it.

On payday, I try to get to work a few minutes early because the first thing I do is sit for five minutes and pay my bills. Once you have a system, it should not take you longer than that. As I pay each bill, I draw a line through it and add a check mark at the end. The payments that come out automatically on a later date I deduct immediately. If I don't record those deductions right away I run the risk of using the money when it wasn't really there for me to use. I don't care if it is only the fifth and US Bank isn't taking their money until the fifteenth. I am going to pay it anyway, so I deduct it now. The money was never mine to use.

I'll tell you how this single mother not collecting any child support, and who signed over her share of the house and took on half of the marital debt in the divorce, paid off $37,500 in debt in three years, one month.

Here is an example of what my budget looks like:

February 5th

          2240 out
          <u>2258 in</u>
            18 left

Rent	900
Car payment	390
US Bank	214
Gas	150
Groceries	150
Butts	150
Merriday	198 (this amount varies)
National Grid	40
<u>Time Warner Cable</u>	<u>48</u>
	2240

The next one looks like this:

February 20th   1341 out
                                      <u>1320 in</u>
                                       - 21 left
                                        <u>18 (last check)</u>
                                        -3

Kohl's	115 (pd. in full)	
Insurance	415	
Gas	150	
Groceries	150	
Butts	80	
Eddie (taxes)	130	I will cut back on groceries
Daniel Y	35	to close this gap!
Verizon	88	
<u>JCPenney</u>	<u>178 (pd. in full)</u>	
	1341	

February 20th   1343. out
                                                   1320. in
                                                    30 left over

Kohl's   115.00
SF Ins.   415.00 $7 left
gas   125.00   √ 60#
groceries   150.00
bills   80.00   put in CB
Eddie (gas)   130.00
Soster (1st)   35.00
Verizon   90.00
JC Penney   178.00 – pd in full
                   1343.00

60 gal. $50 gas
150 gal. $100 gro.
          35 loan
          25 girls

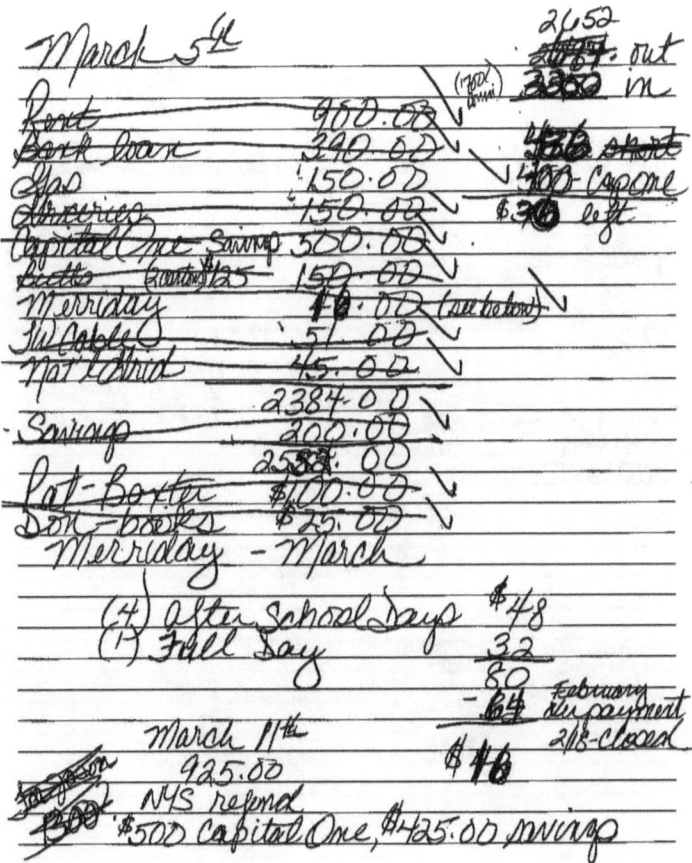

3240 in 2

March 5th

2652
~~2757~~ out
3300 in

Rent 900.00
Bank loan 290.00
Gas 150.00
America 150.00
Capital One Savings 500.00
Debt 150.00
Merriday .... 48.00 (out to loan)
TW Cable 51.00
Nat'l Grid 45.00
                2384.00
- Savings 200.00
                2584.00
Pat - Books $100.00
Don - books $25.00
Merriday - March

(4) After School Days $48
(1) Full Day   32
                      80
                    - 64 February
                         no payment
March 11th   2/8 closed
    925.00 $16
    NYS refund
    $500 Capital One, $425.00 savings

$2384 in w/ bonus

March 20th   1952.00 - out
                                              1935.00 - in

Kohls   189.00   pd. in full $18   8 left
St. Ins.   48.00
gas   150.00   3.75% $ 1820 - salary
groceries   150.00   tax $ 1890 - gross bonus
butts $65.02 - $1000 net bonus
Donald Trust   35.00
Verizon   88.00 $2485 net income
Cap One   155.00 $1000 concert trip
                 132.00   1985 in jr bills
Mercedy $96.00
Savings   100.00
                1452.00

                    $18 overage this period

Capital One $2200 on 3/7
NYS refund   600 payment on 3/20
             = 100
             1500 Cap. One balance

I put notes all over my sheet as I need to. It starts out nice and neat and as things come up, I make adjustments. If I have a co-pay that I received a statement for, I know I need to make room in next month's budget for it. I had to pay my accountant Eddie and although I got a whopping tax return, he just wasn't in the budget to pay before now. Eddie and my doctor's office aren't going to charge me a late fee, and I am not going to take advantage of that, but I find it perfectly ok to send the doctor's co-pay check out at the end of the month. My bills are down to a science now. My car needing an oil change doesn't sneak up and bite me. I see the little sticker in the window; I know when I'm going to have to put regular maintenance money into my car. I plan ahead for it.

My budget used to look a lot worse. It used to be filled with many more bills with much smaller portions being rationed out of my paycheck to get them paid. I used to make a lot less money. I take a few minutes once every few months when it really sinks in how far I've come, to thank my boss for gainful employment. I thank God every single day. My boss comes in a distant second.

When I first started a new life at the end of 2009 my annual salary was significantly less than I currently earn. I made a change and was hired by another agent that saw my value. We negotiated a sweet deal and that is one reason I am so thankful for him. Suddenly my base salary in itself was what I previously made for both salary and commission combined. I still made the same commission for busting my butt as in my prior office, but that bump in base made me want to work as hard as I could for my new boss. That and I wanted him to be satisfied with the decision he made to pay me what he pays me. I will be the last person to cause someone to feel that they took a chance on me and I let them down, thus ruining it for any future chances they may take on someone. I wanted to prove myself to him and I believe I have. I'm still employed and his production is still growing upward.

Let's get back to the budget now. I don't want to harp on the smoking thing but I told you that my ways of getting out of debt are going to be based on my personal stories and this one just can't be avoided. This book is no public service announcement, but some of my choices are going to parallel the choices that many other people make about what they want to waste their money on. For you it may be the casino, but I certainly hope not. There is no limit to what you can gamble away in one unlucky day. I can only smoke so much in a day. It's never going to cost me my rent or my mortgage for a pack of butts, but the loss that can occur from lotto and gambling is limitless.

I believe it is much worse for me to smoke than most other people out there. Why? Because I can see exactly what I waste each month by actually budgeting almost $300 of my hard earned money on a product that is slowing killing me. Most people don't write down their expenditures like I do. They just keep buying them without realizing what they are wasting their money on. Try it with coffee if you find yourself going through the drive-thru every morning. The fact that I now see it, allow it, and budget it for it, sickens me. When I am ready, that money will go in the bank, too. It's like I said earlier, there is money for whatever you want there to be money for.

I do spend quite a bit less on my dirty habit now, because my mother lives in Pennsylvania and I discovered that the same cigarettes that are $10 per pack in NY are $63 per carton in Pennsylvania. That's $63 after tax! Once I got my bills paid down to a really low point and Capital One was paid off, I started "investing" in cigarettes.

I can't believe I'm teaching you how to save money on cigarettes, but it is one of my examples and it's a fact. I don't smoke a pack a day. I'm just over half a pack, but at $10 per pack and buying a pack almost every day, I was spending $300 per month. Imagine how much sooner I could have paid off a bill, but let's not focus on that right now.

I bought three cartons of cigarettes on my freshly paid Visa card for $189. Those thirty packs surely lasted me at least a month and then some. I'd be back down to see my mother or have her visit before I ran out. I then took the $150 I normally budgeted to pay my capital one bill and added $39 from my budgeted $150 that was earmarked for butts, and paid off the balance. I had $11 left over from this check, and that next paycheck, I saved the $150 I would have used for the butts. I still had no balance on my credit card and I used that savings to dump on another balance to get it paid.

It saves me $120 per month to buy them in Pennsylvania. Last time I checked, I wasn't breaking any laws because I wasn't bringing them back for other people or selling them, I just picked them up as I was passing through.

Now, my mother hates that I smoke. She has never smoked a day in her life, but she knows I'm going to smoke anyway, so I actually got her to bring them to me if she's visiting. She only does it because she knows she's saving me a fortune and the only thing worse than my smoking, is my smoking at a cost greater than it has to be.

More money for what you want

I managed to pay for a trip for my girls and I to go to Aruba in February 2012. I called to wish my very dear friend, Paul a happy birthday in September 2011, and he invited us to join him and his wife at their condo.

They would be there the entire month of February and after we figured out what week his family would be visiting, I scheduled my week. I saved a ton of money by planning an eight-day trip due to the days the airlines have higher rates and my friend was fine with us being there one day longer. It was a difference of $1600 on airfare by changing the date. I scrimped and saved every extra dime I could get my hands on because now that I had a deadline to face, the race was on.

My passport had expired 2 years prior and my daughters didn't have one at all. Guess what Santa brought for Christmas that year? You guessed it, passports. Don't get me wrong, Santa didn't actually bring passports but my very understanding children knew it was not going to be a huge Christmas.

They were so excited about the trip that if all they had gotten were passports they would have been thrilled. It cost me almost $475 for the three of us. My airfare went on my debit card as soon as I had the funds, and I opened a second account at the bank to be used just for trip savings with every penny I could add to it. Once the money was in there, it didn't get touched for any reason whatsoever. This required discipline, discipline, and more discipline.

I squirrelled away every penny I could until I had enough to pay for the passports. Once that was done, the budget tightened even further and every extra penny went into the vacation fund. Our flight was so fittingly on Valentine's Day and by then I had saved up $1200 for spending money. Now that may not seem like a lot to people who blow $3000 on restaurants and other extravagances while they are away. I had the mindset and impressed that mindset unto my children that the vacation was the point of being there. Not to get there and see how fancy we could be.

My friends Paul and Lucy, who have the condo where we were staying are probably two of the most successful people I know, both financially and compassionately. Lucy worked at one of the highest levels of the IRS you could go, and Paul was a corporate executive, CFO, CPA, and every other initial you could put after his name. They are like second parents to me. I worked for Paul when I was 17 at the same company where I met Stu and he hasn't been able to get rid of me since. They are my extended family.

My point is that Paul has a most impressive stock portfolio, money in the bank and a nest egg that will support his entire family down to the grandchildren for their entire lives. Guess what they do for dinner? They eat in. Lucy cooks. For lunch, we had sandwiches we packed to take to the beach. If Paul didn't finish his sandwich one day, Lucy gave it him the next day. We ate leftovers for dinner with what remained from the previous two days. We food shopped and very rarely ate at restaurants. They are the epitome of what I am trying to teach you in this book. Just because you can spend money doesn't mean you have to. Paul and Lucy choose what to spend their money on and they choose wisely.

I was afraid I'd waste my money in Aruba so as soon as I arrived at the condo I immediately went down to the tourism desk in the lobby with my girls. We chose what activities we would do each day and I paid for them in advance for the week. We went horseback riding, to the butterfly farm, snorkeled off the back of a catamaran and went on a semi-sub to view an underwater ship-wreck. On Sunday we went to Catholic mass and toured the ancient cemetery. It was so beautiful. We souvenir shopped for everyone on our lists. Our days were spent at the beach when there weren't scheduled events. The girls played at one of the three pools our condo had and we had an event-filled eight days.

I took Paul and Lucy and a few of their friends to dinner one night. I had to give the waiter my credit card during dinner so no one would know. They would have never let me pay and I wanted to thank them for hosting us. That was probably the biggest purchase I made all trip and well worth it. I was able to spend awesome moments with my daughters exploring. We saw the natural bridge, the light-house and all the wonderful things we could fit in while we were there. My point to this whimsical tale is that when it was time to go home, I still had $480 cash from what I brought to spend. We skimped on nothing. We just spent it wisely and I was able to impart these lessons unto my daughters. I didn't borrow against my 401k to take a vacation like I see so many of my friends do.

When we returned, just this once, I didn't take that extra money and put it on a bill. I splurged on an inexpensive Kodak all-in-one photo printer, extra ink on sale of course, and lots of paper so I could print out all the photos we took. When my girls look back at their childhood, they aren't going to feel monetarily rich, but they also aren't going to feel cheated either. I believe they are going to appreciate everything they had. That's a richness money can't buy.

If you put your mind to it, there is money for whatever you want there to be money for. The best thing happened before I left. I had hoped to bring more spending money and I was waiting for my direct deposit tax return. It didn't show up until the day after I left so I had no access to the $9000 return waiting in my account when I arrived home.

Thank God for that or who knows how differently I would have behaved. I do thank God for little things like that every day. He knows what's best and I have to trust that. All I can do is keep plugging along doing the right thing and everything falls into place in little ways. Don't think I walked out of the duty free shop without a few cartons of cigarettes for home, though. Old habits die hard!

Christmas in August

Right now, I'm going to discuss how I shop for Christmas. I do not participate in Black Friday and I never have. I believe it to be a disgrace and I avoid it at all cost.

Besides, I'm usually done shopping for Christmas by Halloween and have everything wrapped by Thanksgiving. Now I know most of you want to hit *me* right now instead of my mother for being skinny. Getting the shopping and wrapping done early leaves me all the time to truly enjoy the holidays for what they are supposed to be.

I shop early because I have to. It's not about the hustle and bustle of shopping and fighting over a flat screen TV that no one on your list really needs, especially you! I can't reasonably come up with the money for Christmas all within a month and not go completely into hock so I start early. Because my kids don't get everything they ask for when they ask for it, I have a pretty good understanding of what they really want for Christmas. They've been asking all year. They don't start picking stuff off the TV at random when some new toy ad comes on. I can weed out what presents will be a waste of money based on the mistakes I've made in the past.

I used to think I had to buy them a lot of things to give them an extra special Christmas because they came from a "broken home". But they really only pay attention to a few of the great things they are looking forward to. The rest is just filler that winds up on the closet shelf as a reminder to me that I could have used that money for something better. Christmas is not about the presents. It's about a birth and family.

They are getting older now, and their gifts are getting more expensive. They've been asking for an iPad and a Wii for two years. Since they asked again for the third year, I figured they must really want it. I can't afford this stuff, so I researched on-line and bought the best tablet that was out there. I went to Wal-Mart.com and bought the Samsung Galaxy 10.1 Note or something, whatever, I don't even know what I bought. I'm not technology savvy.

What do I see before my wandering eyes? A refurbished version at a fraction of the price! Now I'm not a fan of refurbished anything because I've experienced what my cell phone company calls "like new" and I've had nothing but problems with refurbished phones.

Wal-Mart guarantees these products to be in perfect working order and with all the money I saved on the price, I invested an extra $35 for the two-year extended warranty. This warranty will cover the tablet if it gets wet, dropped, or if some idiot steps on the screen and breaks it. By the time the warranty is up, there will have been ten more of these in newer versions anyway. I put that on my credit card in August. It was $179 with free shipping because I spent more than $100. I had it paid off by September. I also purchased the Wii from the same site because they had a bundle that no one could believe I got for the price. It came with seven games and good games, not the cheesy choices, plus an extra controller and some type of nun chuck controller for under $200. I got free shipping again.

I bought that in September and had it paid off by the end of that month. The rest of their presents were smaller items that I bought each time I got a paycheck because I had a list of exactly what I was going to buy for each of them and exactly what it would cost. Then I switched my Safelite Glass pad around and squeezed out extra money from each check to come up with the funds by cutting back on groceries, gas, and anywhere I could. I would pay a little less on the balances that I normally send chunk payments to and use that cash for gifts.

I did struggle back and forth and almost made the horrific decision to buy a second tablet so each of my little monsters had their own. After all I got such a great price, didn't I?

I mulled that one over for quite a while and I'm so glad I decided against it. It would have been overkill and I would have spent almost $200 on something that they didn't really need. My girls will never know what they missed out on and they are so happy with what they got. See, even I have to talk myself out of stupid mindless spending. Just because it's a good deal doesn't mean you have to get it.

I also bought a lot of stuff from Ebay. I have given and received some great things as gifts from Ebay. My oldest daughter showed an interest in knitting but to get her started would be costly. I scoured Ebay for the best deals on bulk yarn, knitting needles and supplies. I bought her an inexpensive but really cute storage box that looks like a miniature travel trunk at Christmas Tree Shops for about $25. I could have gotten one for less, but this one was cute, and as I've told you, I don't cut back as much where my girls are concerned. I will do without so they don't have to. I bought her a book from Barnes & Noble that teaches beginners how to knit and it came with an instructional DVD.

I don't buy them mindless toys that they will grow bored of or games that require sitting in front of the computer for hours to play. Knitting is a healthy outlet and it will teach her something that works her mind and keeps her occupied. I got both of my daughters' books that were on their lists because they read every single night before bed. I would call it a requirement in my house but they love it so much it's more of a pleasure. Every night they read and pray. Just before the holiday season really kicks in for everyone, is just about the time my girls' and I eat more soup. They think it's because its winter, not because I'm buying them stuff with the grocery money.

I fit Christmas into my budget. I don't fit my budget into Christmas. I am a very smart shopper and when I see something on sale that I know I have to buy at some point anyway, I get it. For the Christmas season I try as hard as I can to debit as many of my purchases as I can out of my checking. Once it's gone, I have to learn to live without it.

I do use my credit card, but I am very careful about what I put on it and for how much because I know what my future checks will be and can adjust accordingly. You will not find me running out and charging up thousands of dollars of stuff to get through the holidays. I hear the horror stories from my friends when the bills come in in January. I am not Scarlet O'Hara that will think about that tomorrow. I live for today and plan for tomorrow accordingly.

I did have a credit card balance left over after Christmas, but it was manageable and that's when tax season comes in to save the day again. Since I pay off more and more debt each year, less and less of my return goes to paying off the previous years' mistakes.

I used my Kohl's card only when they mailed me coupons, and doubled up to use them during sales, and got a ton of my other presents there. That in turn earned me more Kohl's cash to go back and use on the rest of the presents I needed. Yes, some of the gifts I gave were purchased for free with Kohl's cash that I earned.

I bought the Monster High Dolls that both my daughters wanted from Kohl's using coupons and Kohl's cash. By the time I was done shopping on the day with early bird discounts, I got those $35 dolls for about $12.

My daughter had been complaining that her pillow was getting flat. I hadn't planned on buying her a pillow for Christmas, but I happened to be at you guessed it, Kohl's, on a particular night when they were having a two-hour super sale. The memory foam pillow that my daughter grabs and holds to her face every time we are in the store, cost $55-60 for the basic one. I can't tell you how many times I told her to put it back because, "I am not paying $55 for a pillow!" That day the pillows were on sale for 50% off, plus the two-hour super sale was advertising that for a two-hour window they were $19.99. I had a 20% off coupon bought her the pillow for $16. I got her the $55 memory foam pillow for $16! I added a $7 Justin Beiber pillow-case that I ordered from a discount catalogue, and she was absolutely thrilled when she opened those two gifts Christmas morning. She thought Mommy was a Rock-star!!!

I got home with my purchase and remembered that I had also bought one of those memory foam pillows for my brother for his birthday in September. He had been in the hospital for an unfortunate extended stay and loves to be surrounded by a ton of soft pillows and blankets.

He kept complaining that he couldn't stand the pillows. Since he was spending his birthday in the hospital, I splurged on one of those memory foam pillows when they were just 50% off. I took my receipt back to Kohl's and told them I wanted a price adjustment. I had just gotten the same pillow for my daughter for $16 and his was $25. Not only did they do the price adjustment, they honored the two-hour super savings and added my 20% off coupon. I don't know how it happened but I wound up with more credit on my Kohl's account than my math calculated and his pillow came out to even less than the $16 that I paid for my daughters.

Be careful though. If you purchase a gift using Kohl's cash, don't give a gift receipt. They will get jammed up if they try to return it because the computer system recalls every discount and method of payment you use when they scan the receipt. Kohl's is so good about returns you never need a receipt anyway. The store will give you the best price it can on a return or an exchange. I've seen the employees do things at the return counter that almost make me feel guilty by the time I walk out because they are so good to me.

I've never shopped in a store that is so accommodating to its patrons. I have rambled on about how you can save a fortune at Kohl's and what wonderful experiences I've had every time I've ever been there. On this particular day, I came right out and told the manager that my experience with her customer service girl would single-handedly be the reason I would never return to Kohl's again. DO NOT MESS WITH MY MONEY OR MY KOHL'S CASH!

I wanted to exchange a $150 comforter set I bought on-line for $150 in different merchandise. I tried to find a bed set that I liked in the store but I just couldn't. I wasn't looking for my money back. I just didn't want to lose the Kohl's Cash that I earned for that purchase. I scoured the store for over an hour to find items I could really use that totaled the same amount. I had done that once before with no problem. Suddenly it was like I was asking for her first-born child! She shot me down, wouldn't let me speak. She kept cutting me off and with such an attitude!

It was my one bad experience at Kohl's and rest assured, once I was done throwing my hissy fit, the manager fixed it and I was better off than I would have been if the cranky girl had just properly helped me to begin with. She tried to tell me that I could only exchange my bed set for one "like" item to keep my Kohl's cash! What? Uhm, no I don't think so.

This girl continued to argue with me even after the manager had rectified the situation. She claimed that she really tried to help me, but that, "I just didn't give her a chance". I went on to tell her that I was not interested in continuing to argue with her, but that she had not, in fact, tried to help me. All she kept telling me was that there was nothing she could do to help me and that it was "impossible" to exchange my items the way I wanted to; it was store policy.

Let's use some common sense, people. The last thing you want to tell someone who is already irate is that they should calm down, or blame them further. My girls were hiding in the toy department and my mother wanted to crawl in a hole. I was shaking because I really hate conflict. My voice trembled as I stood my ground and let this girl know that I deserve to be treated with respect. Standing up for myself is a fairly new concept. I will vehemently race to the rescue or defense of someone else, but I tend to let people walk all over me.

It angered me further then. I felt like she was accusing me of being unreasonable and she had the impression that I always behave like that. I assure you that I do not go into stores yelling and shaking at sales people.

In fact, I'm extra nice because I know if I strike up a conversation and treat them well, I'm going to be privy to that secret coupon they have behind the register. It works every time. I am well aware that you catch more flies with honey than you do with vinegar.

To save more money on the stuff for Christmas that secretly adds up, I buy my wrapping paper for $1 per roll. It may be annoying to work with this crappy, sheer paper when wrapping presents, but it gets torn up and thrown in the garbage anyway so why would I spend $3.59 or more on the good heavy-duty stuff?

I also don't buy expensive greeting cards. I tear a little piece of extra wrapping paper, fold it in half and tape it to the box with the name of whom the gift is for and from. I do buy cards for occasions when I need to, but unless I've completely messed up somebody's life royally, I'm not spending $4 on a greeting card.

There are three types of wrapping paper in my house at Christmas for the girls. They each get one type of paper that I use only for that child's gifts, then there's the Santa paper. I will not buy gift tags and risk them recognizing my handwriting like I did when I was a kid, and it's a good way to not give someone the wrong gift. My oldest daughter usually picks something with animals on it and my youngest picks something goofy. I use this for the gifts that come from Mommy. When they are not with me, I buy the paper that has Santa on it, hide it, and use it for the presents that Santa brings. A simple little initial for what child is getting those will let me know who is supposed to open what on Christmas morning.

When I gave them the tablet and the Wii, I told them that I saw Santa bringing them and he wanted me to let them know that each present was to be shared with the other child. They were so thrilled to get such great gifts that they play with them together just fine. After all, I wasn't buying two tablets or two Wii's. Don't get me wrong, I definitely need to limit how long each one uses the tablet or there will be unrest in my house. I have that down to a system, and we all get along famously.

Who am I kidding? As I just typed that last line, I heard the two of them yelling at each other, "It's my turn! You've been on it the whole time."

The solution to that problem is setting the timer on the microwave and when it goes off, the other gets a turn. That's the end of the story. If the arguing ensues, I take it away completely and make them both sorry they fought over something so silly.

I was getting the girls ready for Daniel to pick them up and take them to church this morning, and as I gave them breakfast and vitamins I saw that I had only six vitamins left. I said, "This is perfect girls. I have enough vitamins for three more days, Monday, Tuesday, and Wednesday". They go to Daniels' on Wednesday. By then I would get paid and buy more.

I immediately write down anything I need on the magnetic pad that sticks to my fridge. That's my shopping list from which I DO NOT waiver. I saw that I had already completed the list and reached my $150 budget. That $150 used to be split over the fifteen days between pay periods but because the cost of everything has gone up so much, I use the whole thing at once now and just make everything last until I get paid again.

I used to do the big shopping for about $125 and leave $25 for the staples that carry us over for the next week, but that doesn't work anymore. I have learned to time the purchase of a gallon of milk so that the majority of it is used on the week that I have the girls the most and the little bit that is left, sits in the back of the fridge where it's colder and waits for their return. It stays fresh and I no longer have to throw out sour milk.

There was either no room for vitamins this week or something had to go. The girls join me while we review the list and they help me decide what we can live without for a week. It goes further in their learning and makes them feel important to be included.

I saw that I had budgeted $13 for mini-sized cartons of soy milk. These are like regular little containers of milk, but my girls really like the soy milk and it doesn't run the risk of having hormones in it. On occasion I buy a case as a treat and to offer some variety. It's expensive, but a case of twelve can last me a month using one per day for each girl's lunch for school. They know that those milks are not to be had at home under any circumstance. They are counted and allocated for school lunches only. Besides, I buy half-gallon containers of the same stuff for them to drink at home in a cup for a fraction of the price.

I looked in the fridge and saw that I still had a box and a half left of the

Capri Sun Roaring Waters pouches that I bought and that would surely last the rest of the month. I asked them if I could take the soy milk off the list and add it to the next list, freeing up $13 to buy other items that we needed sooner. They were so on board with it. They love their vitamins and by the time I buy the soy milk, I will probably have another dollar-off coupon for it. Then I get my little thrill knowing that I'm being rewarded for waiting. I get so frustrated when I buy something without a coupon just to find a coupon for it a few days later. Ahhh, it's the little things in life.

I also needed pancake syrup that costs $2.50 and the vitamins are about $6 without a coupon. My grocery list was at $168.50 before coupons. I have $13.50 in coupons, bringing my list total to $155.00. I know I'm $5 over, but I can buy a few less cold cuts, fresh veggies, or fruit and lower my list using price-by-the-pound items to my advantage. By getting ½ lb. of cheese instead of a pound, or by buying a little less broccoli or string beans, I can lower my bottom line by the $5 that I over budgeted.

I know all these crazy little stories may seem like too much work, but the whole idea of this book is to show you how change in little ways can completely morph your everyday thought process. Don't forget that I managed to pay for an entire eight-day trip to Aruba for three people with cash that I squeezed out my existing budget. If you don't think these little ways will help, tell that to the creditors that got just got paid 37,500!

I told you that this process would take patience and sacrifice and I wasn't joking. This is like an extreme makeover for your finances, and only good can come out of it. I loosen the purse strings a little here and there when things get better, but because I have developed healthier spending habits in the process, I don't go crazy anymore. Read on to see how tight and meticulous it gets.

When I added the syrup and vitamins to the list but removed the soy milk, my total before groceries came down to $163.50. Take off the $13.50 I have in coupons, and I just brought myself back on budget. This adds up to more money than you can possibly imagine over time, and by the end of the month I can squeeze an extra $50 into my wallet. Scratch that, I don't carry money. I can keep an extra $50 in my checking account. Can you use an extra $50 in your account?

Most of the women reading this next section are going to hunt me down in a dark alley, and the men reading the book will cheer and almost force their wives to read *just this section*.

One of the biggest areas I am able to save money on is maintenance. Oh here we go, no one is going to want to hear or read this part!

I do not tan. I don't lie in a tanning bed or get spray-tanned. I do not get my nails done, ever, and I color my own hair with a $7 box of color that I buy with a coupon when the budget allows.

The girls I work with get their nails done either every week or every other week, I'm not sure. They have tips and fill-ins or overlays. They have their hair cut, colored, frosted (yes, frosted) about every four to six weeks. I haven't even had my hair cut since November, 2011. My hair looks pretty good for as little as I do to it and for it. I eat pretty healthy food when I'm not scouring for candy, so that helps. I was also blessed with a much better head of hair than my mother got, so I do have naturally decent locks. Do not confuse this with me saying the maintenance doesn't get done. It does, I assure you, and I still stop traffic when I walk out of the house. I am always primped and well groomed.

This is where it's going to get really ugly. I save an absolute fortune on products. I buy VO5 for $0.79 per bottle each for shampoo and conditioner. I just can't bring myself to buy the salon stuff at $28 a bottle or even $7 a bottle. I've compared the ingredient labels and they're just about the same. I'm sure the salon stuff is better, I'm not going to deny it, but at this point I am not willing to give up that money to buy better stuff that doesn't have enough of an impact on the final result.

I recently bought eight bottles of VO5 because I had two coupons for it. I didn't even think you could get a coupon for an item that was already so cheap. If I bought four bottles, I'd save $1.00. The price normally fluctuates between $0.79 and $0.99, but at the time I had the coupon it was $0.79. Score!

I paid $0.79 multiplied by eight, which is $6.32 for all you mathematicians out there, and I used both $1.00 coupons, totaling $4.32 for eight bottles of really nicely scented shampoos and matching conditioners. I won't have to buy those items for many months to come. Take a look at what you spend on that stuff and see if there isn't somewhere to cut back.

I have been using the same styling products since junior high school when they came on the market. I put a little 'roo in my do every day. I just can't find a better product than the Aussie line. I use the coupons and I stock up on Sprunch Spray, Instant Freeze, and anti-frizz because I kind of have curly hair.

I had bouncy ringlet curls before I had my first daughter and they were really low maintenance. It went straighter after I had my second daughter. Now it's somewhere in between straight, curly, and frizzy. I know you're thinking it's because I buy the cheap stuff, but au contraire mon frère. I have experimented with the "better" salon products and have found absolutely no difference in how my hair turns out. Aussie fixes that.

I've been given free samples or gift cards for Christmas that I've used to buy the best stuff out there and there is no hairspray on the market that works better for me than Instant Freeze. I will test it against yours any day of the week. I have also been using the same razors for at least three years. Yupper. I got a three-pack of those really good Venus razors in my stocking and I swear it may have been when I was still married.

They're not even the new ones that come with the moisture block thing on them. I am talking about the original Venus razors from when Jewel came out with the song that they used in the commercial, so three years isn't event accurate. I just gave everyone an unwelcomed flash back and grossed you out simultaneously!

I am down to only having one left because I think I lost one in a move somewhere, but they still work and I swear that I don't cut myself. I supplemented them with one of the $1.00 packs of ten razors that really are crap I admit, but I stop using them when they rust. Yes, they rust. I bet no one has ever kept and used a razor long enough for it to rust.

I warned you that what I do is extreme. Add up what you spend on all the products and services I've just referred to and I bet some of you spend over $100 per month on that stuff. No one is saying you have to quit cold turkey, but I bet there is a place for you to cut back even a little.

I should correct that I don't ever get my nails done. Once or twice a year, I will either splurge on a pedicure, or my boyfriend will insist I get one because I have very painful feet. He knows that a massaging pedicure will make them feel better and lift my spirits. Having him rub my feet doesn't always cut it. I agree that sometimes you need to just go and allow yourself something nice or you'll go crazy. Then I come home and complain that I do a better job or I cry because they made fun of me.

Let's not get confused about what my hands, hair and feet look like. I am very well put together - I just do it myself. I give myself a really good pedicure and avoid having to bear my dogs to the population that makes fun of them in their native language right in front of me. You know what I'm talking about. I don't need to pay good money, plus a tip, to be mortified while I'm having some type of treatment done because they're talking to the girl sitting next to me and making fun of my toes. It's obvious!

I have large feet and growing up I was forced to squeeze them into smaller shoes because no one sold size 12 back when I was 14 years old. If there was a specialty store that carried them, my mother couldn't afford to pay the ridiculous prices they would charge anyway. I've had foot surgery several times to try to correct the damage that was done to my feet. The damage is from a combination of growing up with shoes that were too small added to what I've done to them as an adult putting them in the worst shoes I can because they are cute or hot, or sexy, or all three.

I fluctuate between a size 10 and 11 now and can find shoes on any rack. After I lost a lot of weight at age 19, I went down a shoe size or two. Guess I had fat feet, too. I also get the best sales because there isn't a huge demand for my size shoe and when they go on clearance, guess whose size is almost always available? Mine. My clod-hoppers get shod in some hot shoes!

I talk with my girlfriends all the time about planning a spa day, but scheduling conflicts have halted the progress. I do like to feel like a girl and I'm not telling anyone out there that they shouldn't get anything done. I'm just saying that there are places to cut back if you really want to get yourself out of the red and into the black. I've been known to splurge on a Brazilian wax now and again, but that's something I just can't do myself, and don't think I haven't tried! Boy, that's a scary thought.

I would love to have a facial or get a massage. That's what I start hinting for around Christmas. I want gift cards to go get the things done that I won't pay for myself. I mention that I would love to get my pores vacuumed so I can stop picking at my face in the mirror every day.

I have a really great girlfriend who during her divorce had no choice but to file for bankruptcy. She was left with a mountain of debt and the bills had gone so far into arrears that making agreements with the credit card companies wasn't an option anymore. I don't fault her for that. She was in a tight spot that both of them caused and she was the one left to clean up the mess.

What I disagree with is the fact that she changed nothing about her habits during or after what she called the most embarrassing time of her life. She hated that she had to answer an attorney for where every penny would come from, afraid they were going to make her hock her engagement ring to offset the judgments.

How did she correct the mess she was in? By continuing to drive through Starbucks THREE TIMES A DAY, having her hair colored, highlighted, lowlighted, blown out, the works.

She actually goes to a salon just to get her hair blow-dried at $50 a pop. She has a manicure and fill-in just about every week, and she is absolutely addicted to pedicures. So much so, that she developed some unsightly foot issues that I won't get into from having them done at places where the water or tubs aren't cleaned properly, yet she still goes!!!!

Her podiatrist told her to lay off the pedicures for a year to fix the condition but she's afraid someone will see her imperfect feet. Uhmmm, I know you wear boots in the winter. Can you compromise and lay off for four to five months for the sake of your health?

Add the cost of spray tanning to the point where I had to have a heart-to-heart sit down with her and tell her she was more than beginning to look like an Oompa Loompa from Willy Wonka's chocolate factory! The total price tag for the tanning is more than she is willing to disclose. I won't even touch on what she spends at Bloomingdale's or Black & White.

My friend likes to go out and have fun with her friends. Why shouldn't she? She is single now and has no children, but it's nothing to her to blow $150 on a night out having drinks several times a week.

I can only say this because she has finally started changing her ways. Her skin color is a more normal shade of golden copper, and most of this was five years ago. She has more recently tightened the purse strings if even just a bit, straightened herself out and she's doing much better. In fact, she's getting ready to buy a house. Good for her. Everyone is so proud of her!

I have the cheapest cell phone plan I can get without worrying about going over my minutes, costing me more. I also researched and found that I am eligible for a 22% corporate discount from my cell phone carrier. That is huge, but I have to be careful not to be "penny wise and pound foolish." I will find that on occasion I cost myself $5 while trying to save a dollar. I think the expression is, "Tripping over dollars to collect pennies".

I have a closet full of beautiful Cache' clothes so I am presentable for work, but when I shop now I buy one dress on clearance instead of walking out with an $800 tab. That might make me look like a rock-star in the eyes of the salesgirl, but feel like a fool in my head. I pick up wardrobe pieces on sale that I can mix and match and that will last through the seasons. I am no longer #11 on Cache's top one hundred customers (based on annual purchases) but I still own most of the clothes. I don't care if I'm not the top spender anymore. My entire outlook is different.

Dessert

Coupons & reduced meat

This is more of a sub-chapter as it relates to the budget but is perfect for dessert. Indulge sparingly. When I food shop, I buy very and I mean very specific quantities of the items on my list. I have an accurate count of what days I have to pack lunch and prepare dinner and I buy no more than what will carry me to the next shopping trip.

I almost never run out of anything. I could say never but then I would jinx myself and next week would run out of milk. When I say I don't run out, that doesn't mean I don't run low. I only buy enough to get by. I am not going to buy so much fresh fruit and fresh vegetables that I am throwing stuff away because it rotted before we could consume it. If I need to make fun, delicious smoothies with the girls because we can't eat the fruit before it turns, they get all excited. I chuckle to myself. Not only do we all get a yummy treat for dessert, Mommy just saved $4 worth of fruit that would have rotted.

Here is where Josh becomes my example. He loves to eat a lot of fresh fruit throughout the week, and good for him. It's healthy. He buys the bulk bag of oranges, the bulk bag of apples and the biggest bunch of bananas he can find.

By the way, the bulk stuff isn't always cheaper and it isn't always the freshest. Check the price per pound before you buy a larger quantity and see who is tricking whom. I have purchased enough bags of bulk apples at a good price only to find the ones in the middle - that I couldn't see no matter how hard I tried to scan the bag - are rotten or bruised.

Josh buys all of this in one shopping trip. He can't possibly eat it all in one week. I've seen what this "fresh" fruit looks like by the end of the week, and I have seen how much of it gets thrown away. That is a huge waste of food and money.

You should be able to gauge how much your family is really going to consume and adjust it until you get it right. Sometimes you may have too much of something, sometimes you'll fall short. Eventually you'll get it down to the science that I have. Don't think I don't suggest or push certain foods onto the girls when they are not going to last much longer. If my daughter wants an apple, I ask her to please have a banana because they aren't going to last another day or two and she gladly has one. If she eats the banana and still wants the apple, she can have one.

We all know how fast a banana can go from green to brown. I buy them when they are still slightly green so I know I have at least a couple of days before we need to seriously start consuming them.

I buy fruits that are in season. Right now we are eating a lot of oranges. During the summer it's plums and nectarines along with watermelon and cantaloupe. In fall, we eat apples. Apples and bananas are all year long fruits, but I supplement them with seasonal fruit so it keeps the kids coming back for more. If I buy a bulk bag of oranges this week, I'm not going to buy a bulk bag of anything else. Instead, I'm filling in with a few choice pieces of other fruit so there is variety - and I save a bundle.

I do the same thing with fresh vegetables. If I don't like the price per pound on an item, I buy it if I need it but I buy less. I use the scales in the produce department to see how much I'm spending and I will put some back to shave the cost off the grocery list. No one at the dinner table is going to notice if I bought one less head of broccoli or ¼ lb. less of string beans or Brussels sprouts. What does get noticed is that by doing that, I have knocked almost $5 off the bottom line.

I am not going to ramble on any more about fruits and vegetables, but the other culprit is cold cuts. Ever experience the smell of a slimy slice of ham or turkey? Cold cuts do not keep well for very long and can be costly. I estimate how many sandwiches I need to make for the week and buy only two, possibly three types of deli meat each week. I fill in with bologna or salami that keep fresher longer than ham and turkey and use the ham and turkey first. I alternate which meats I buy each week so my daughter doesn't get bored with her sandwiches. If I am going to splurge, I will allow her Roast Beef as a treat if it's really rare, and of course, on sale.

Josh comes into play here again. He buys five to six different types of deli meat plus two to three kinds of cheese in one shopping trip and buys a pound or two of each! I get completely grossed out when I attempt to make a sandwich and everything is moldy or just pungent. Cold cuts at that rate cost him over $35-40 for that little trip. I pay $9 per week for cold cuts and interchange it with egg salad, and tuna that thankfully my daughter loves, especially with the little bits of celery I add in for her. My whole point is that these are the easy ways to save a fortune on groceries and cause so much less waste of really good food.

I have one vegetarian daughter, and one who comes running at the smell of meat roasting. I like to give each of my children what they like and meat is extremely expensive. The veggie meats can be equally as expensive but because I only have the three of us to feed, I manage. You may have to alter what I do if your family is larger.

My meat eater loves pork, lamb, steak and all the good meats. I shop in the meat department by color. Yes by color. My eyes only follow the bright orange stickers that read "reduced for quick sale". It's the same stuff that was full price the evening before but today it's reduced. Don't confuse the stickers with "Manager's Special" or "Todays' Special". Those are usually not the deal you are hoping for.

Let me clarify, please. I DO NOT buy rotten meat. If there is so much as an iota of question, I don't buy it. I have gotten really expensive lamb chops that have two days left for sale and stuffed chicken breasts with feta cheese, walnuts and sun-dried tomatoes for a fraction of the price. No orange stickers? Then there is no meat purchased this week. My girls love rice and beans with veggies, too.

Wegmans makes one and two-person portioned gourmet meat dishes that go right in the oven in the tray. I buy as many as I can and freeze them as soon as I walk through the door. I use them sparingly and when my daughter gets to enjoy those, I get a big thank you. I can't always get those dishes so I only cook them occasionally. I save them until I know I can get more and rotate the stock in the freezer. When I say no orange stickers, no meat, it doesn't mean we go hungry.

These orange sticker deals are perfect for two reasons. First, I get to eat what the people who have more money get to eat at a much lower price. Secondly, I am sometimes exhausted when I get home from work and don't have the energy to put a big meal together. I can grab one of these "fancy" premade entrees out of the freezer, pop it in the oven, and by the time it's done, I have made my side dishes and my older daughter's meat alternative.

Another cheap, easy alternative to a big dinner in our house is what we call "veggie helper". Yes, I make Hamburger Helper for my girls about once a month. I substitute veggie crumbles for the ground beef. I buy the whole grain hamburger helper and it is enough to feed the three of us a light dinner. I use a coupon to buy three boxes of Hamburger Helper and they usually are on sale at three boxes for $3.98. The veggie crumbles are $3.69 a bag, and in the end I feed us dinner for $5.51 if you include the cost of the milk I add in.

It's cooked in fifteen minutes because I don't have to brown and drain the meat. It's low fat and a healthier alternative and cleanup is easy too. Doing this once every month or so saves me a good bit from the budget and it all adds up. I'm not telling you what to eat or how to cook. I don't want this book to go in that direction. These are just examples of how I live and what I do on a day-to-day basis that saves me enough money to keep me chipping away at my bills.

Did you know that if you take one bag of frozen cauliflower at $0.99 per bag and mix half of that bag with one package of boxed cauliflower and cheese sauce you can stretch it to feed three people? Those boxes are more cheese than vegetables and there is never enough in them to feed more than one person. Don't make multiple boxes, just add a plain bag to one box with cheese sauce and see how much more you get. It's just as cheesy, too.

This works with broccoli, spinach and any other type of vegetable with sauce in the box. I buy them with a coupon when they are on sale and pick up store brand vegetables that are almost always $0.99 per one-pound bag.

Don't make the mistake of buying the vegetable that steam in the bag. They cost more per package and have only 12 ounces verses 16 ounces. The real trick is that you can steam whatever you want in whichever bag. They're both plastic bags. The only difference is that for one dollar less, the ones I buy don't come with a fancy seam that tears open and burns you if you don't do it right.

Coffee, Espresso, Cappuccino

Delay of gratification

We live in an instant gratification society and I'm part of it too now and then, but I have learned the hard way that it's almost never worth it. You have to treat yourself to a little something once in a while or you'll go insane. We are human and it is in our nature to desire things…things we don't yet have, things other people already have, the newest thing, the latest thing, or the flashiest thing.…

My ex-husband (poor Daniel, here I am picking on him again) would come home from work irritated because his boss was a jerk (his boss really was a jerk). He'd complain and wonder why everything had to be so hard and ask what he was working so hard for if we were always broke?

I had to explain to him, sometimes more gently than others depending on how bad his mood was, and sometimes pretty frankly, hitting him square between his eyes.

I'd tell him, "because you had four children and they cost money. Because all through your twenties you burned through your money, and even now instead of saving to buy something, you buy it instantly then try to figure out how to pay for it later.

I would tell him to plan for his future! I told him the problem is "if you do that too much and too often, you are left with too many purchases that add up to huge bills that start to swallow you up, overwhelm you, and kill you with interest. No matter how much you pay on the bills, the balance still keeps growing because you keep spending."

I explained to him that we were paying for a life we already lived. I told him we were paying for the dinners we ate out the month before because it was too hot to cook on the second floor and we didn't have air conditioning. Even though we couldn't afford to, we went out to eat. Then when we got to the restaurant, we got appetizers, drinks, dessert, and you know what happened next. The bills came and a simple dinner out just cost over $100. I'm not blaming Daniel for this. You didn't have to ask me twice to go out to eat so I wouldn't have to cook in a hot apartment. I was on board the run-away debt freight train, I just didn't complain about the debt because I knew why we had no money.

Do that a few times a month and you can't wonder why you owe hundreds or thousands of dollars on credits cards. Then your normal, same sized paycheck keeps coming in (if you're lucky) and it quickly becomes too short to cover the bills. You start paying smaller premiums, closer to the minimums thinking that in a few months you'll catch up and start sending more. You're using more of the paycheck to send out the bills, so by three days after you get paid you're broke and again relying on the cards to get you through until you get paid again. That one big run-on sentence is the true reason all of us wind up in over our heads in debt. You'll never get caught up again until you reverse it. So many people have it backwards.

My ex-husband is the perfect example of having it backwards. He makes a good living. He struggles but makes an average wage, probably considered true middle class. He gets his salary every Friday direct deposit. Now you already know that he likes to treat himself because it's his reward for all of his hard work, so the deposit is made and he is off and running. This behavior was the basis for many a fight during our marriage.

Daniel believes that because he is in sales, his attire is important to impress people so they think he is successful and good at what he does. This will make them buy more from him, in turn making him more money. One time when he got paid he went to Macy's (this is a true story) and bought himself the $100 Ed Hardy "Lucky in Love" cologne. Not just the cologne mind you, the gift set because it was a bargain at $100. "Lucky in love?" Really? Did I mention he's my ex-husband? Maybe that's why he sees himself as lucky.

When I asked how he thought he could afford it since he was griping about being broke the very day before, he said buying it was justified because it was necessary for work; he is in sales and needs to smell good. I think a good shower using a fresh-scented soap will bring you the same result, but his budget is his own now, and not something I need to worry myself over anymore.

What he does is backwards because when he is done buying the luxuries and extras, there isn't enough money left to pay the bills. You can't spend money on things you want and try to make what's left over fit the bills. It's the other way around. So instead of buying what you want first, budget to pay your bills first, then use what's left over (if there is any) to buy something you want.

Pay attention, because this is a hint on how to do it, and I just slipped it right in there. You didn't see it coming. Now that's a novel idea. By golly, pay your bills first and then if there is anything left over, use it for expensive cologne, or shoes, or Starbucks or a manicure, or lunch from the deli one day.

What happens when there isn't enough to buy everything you want? You have used your paycheck to pay all of the bills you racked up buying stuff before you've earned the money to do so and there's nothing left.

Here's hint two - don't buy it. Wait until your next paycheck or the next. Seriously, are we such spoiled brats that we can't wait a few weeks or months, or even years for something that we <u>think</u> we truly need and just can't live without?

I think I just thought of a new chapter to add in the end. Learning the difference between want and need. If we truly want something, it's worth waiting for. It's worth working for, and earning.

Over time, you actually become backwards, like being upside down on a loan because you've rolled too many older loans into a new one to get a new car. I'll use the amount of $17,000. That's not an expensive tag for a new car, but $700 for 72 months on that amount is ridiculous, wouldn't you say? You think the dealer cares if you have a $700 car payment for 72 months for a $17,000 car? No, he just sold you a car and you let him. If you can't afford it, don't buy it.

I'm not making this stuff up. I write the insurance for clients on these purchases every day. I can't even offer them a better refinance on it. When they tell me they are paying 23.99% APR, yes 23.99, I know their credit is so bad that I won't do them the disservice of running it again. Don't even get me started on how I think it should be illegal to charge that much for interest. I don't know how some sales people sleep at night, but if there is a fool out there willing to pay it, then who am I to judge? Everybody has to make a living, I guess.

Exercise some self-discipline. I am a firm believer in delay of gratification.

If I want something badly enough I will save for it. Half the time I realize I don't even want it anymore by the time I can buy it. On the occasion that I still really want what I have saved for, I'm not worried about how I'm going to pay for it. I don't have to feel guilty thinking that I shouldn't have. I appreciate, treasure and love those purchases even more.

Children don't understand that these days. They get what they want, when they want it and they grow up not understanding what disappointment and what, "No" means. It's not a great way for parents to prepare them for the real world - unless they find a career that lets Mommy come to work with them every day to make sure they are coddled.

That may sound harsh but I see it all the time through my friends' children's behavior and the kids that come into my office with their parents. I keep a bead table in my office to occupy the younger children when I need to meet with parents about more than just car insurance. I cannot fully comprehend nor can they, what their proper life insurance needs are when their three-year-old child is crumbling pop tarts and throwing them around my office. I am amazed at the lack of discipline nowadays. I want to step in and correct that child then scold the parent for not doing it.

I mentioned earlier that my girls really do thank me for the meals I prepare for them. I get them hyped up; I get them excited. I know what their likes and dislikes are and although I don't offer them a menu, I plan my meals around healthy nutritious food that they love.

The delay part comes in because they have requests for different foods now and then and if the list is already made they know they have to wait until the next list starts.

Can you tell me your kids would get excited about fruit and cream variety oatmeal? Mine do, because normally I don't buy Quaker. I buy Wegman's brand because they sell two boxes for $4 but they don't carry fruit and cream. Quaker is $2.50-$3.00 per box. The dollar that I save buys a 4-pack of Hunt's snack pack pudding for their lunch. When I get a Quaker coupon for $1.00 off, I'll buy two and get them for the same price as the store brand. Then they are thrilled!

I pick a unique fruit almost every shopping trip and when they request Star fruit at $2 each or a Mango that costs 3/$5 (I only buy one), they know it must be off-set by an inexpensive fruit like bananas or apples. They get excited that after one day of apples or bananas in their lunch they get to look forward to sliced Star fruit or a mango.

My girls are not permitted to help themselves to what's in the fridge without asking. That is for several reasons. The first being that I'm not going to have them gorge on mindless snacking between meals only to be too full to eat at mealtime. That causes a snowball of wasted food at dinner and obesity in children.

The other reason is because if I don't keep a strict inventory of what's on hand, I can't properly plan my grocery list and keep on budget. If I allowed them to eat whatever they wanted and I had no idea what's left, I'd have nothing in the fridge to pack for their lunches. Do you have any idea how much of your food cost goes to waste because something got finished that you didn't know about?

Think about how many times you went to grab something to drink or eat and found when you opened the fridge, what was full or unopened the day before was completely gone? It goes beyond frustrating that you now can't enjoy something that you were looking forward to, to wondering how you're going to replace it.

I remember my brother eating an entire rack of par-boiled spareribs when we were kids. My mother took them out to defrost to feed our family of 6 and they had vanished off the counter. They weren't even fully cooked. She kept asking where they went and truthfully my brother ate so much that he really couldn't remember even downing them. We're not talking about munchies, short-term memory loss either because that didn't come until years later. My brothers and I just ate what we wanted without thinking about it.

My mother screamed and yelled but wound up crying because she had nothing to replace it with for dinner and there wasn't money to go out and buy more, or order in for that matter.

When I get the items on my grocery list, I get my girls excited about it. I will call them at Daniel's and tell them. I make a game of it. By this point you're probably thinking I run my house like a military camp, but that's ok. If you met my girls you'd realize that I don't get it all right, but I get a lot of it right. Daniel and my girls are awesome. I call them and say, "Guess what Mommy got at the groooccery stoooorrre". They go crazy and ask, "What! What!"

It could be something simple like a new flavored peanut butter or Cottage Cheese. I start listing all thing fun things I got like a totally new flavor of pudding from the Hunt's Bakery Shop Line and they are wild with delight over the idea of cupcake flavored pudding. This pudding is $1 for a four-pack and it's healthy. They have to wait to come back from Daniel's to enjoy the mini baby bell cheese that I finally found room in my budget for because I had a coupon.

I do the same thing for me, except my gratification is delayed every week and will be for quite some time longer. I do without so they don't have to.

If I can delay the gratification of a simple pleasure like jumbo shrimp, I mean colossal shrimp for my daughter, for over a month because of the cost, do you know how easy it is to get my children to patiently wait for a new bike or that American Girl Doll I mentioned? They don't even realize they're waiting. They have just learned to believe that if they want something, it is worth waiting for.

I'm not tricking them. I'm just not spoiling them. I'm teaching them in little ways that they can't have what they want right away. It is preparing them and me for when they hit high school and want the latest designer clothes or the day they ask me for a car. By then they will have jobs and buy their own cars like I did when I was 17. Nothing was ever handed to me and I wouldn't trade that part of my childhood for anything.

All of this ties right into my budget and how I was able to get out of debt. If I didn't tighten the purse strings and go on this incredibly depraved budget, I'd have kept on putting these things on credit cards. I would never have brought the balances down. They would have just kept creeping up.

My daughter will see something in a store and ask if the price is a lot. "Mommy, is $4 a lot of money?" I answer with a question, "Do you have $4?" When she replies that she does not, then I respond back and tell her that if you don't have $4 then it's a lot. If something costs more than you have then, "Yes, Sweetheart, it's a lot."

My girls put any checks, cash, or collective money they get into their piggy banks and with my approval may spend it on something sensible. That may be a toy, but they will think long and hard about how much they want that toy. If it's a ridiculous purchase, I just shut the whole thing down. They don't argue. Most times, I let them buy books or a little treat, but when my older daughter wants a $4 book that will help her earn more Moshi Monsters then she can pay for it herself. I pay the $5.95 monthly membership. If she wants more, it falls on her.

It's a great idea to teach kids and show them what happens and what they have left when they watch their own money dwindle away. I ask them very poignant questions about what they want to purchase and gently guide or suggest something else bigger that they had their eye on. Nine times out of ten, they'd rather save for that bigger item and wait. Then they forget or realize they don't really want what they thought they did to begin with.

My girls are adorable sometimes and they tug at my heartstrings when I tell them I cannot take them to dinner this week because I get paid next week. They offer up their piggy banks and tell me that they'll pay for it. I am on the right track to teaching them fiscal responsibility for when they are older and have to make these decisions themselves.

If you try these ideas, even some of them, you will see a difference in your cash flow. Try putting your fist down and tell your kids you want to try a project for a month. No one takes anything from the fridge without asking. Then you decide if they really need to eat it. See how much less you spend on groceries that month or how much easier it is to keep your cabinets stocked if it isn't a free-for-all in the kitchen. Don't just say, "Yes" when they ask or that will defeat the purpose of the project.

Nuts

OCD – Embrace It

I have OCD if you haven't already figured that out by now, and it is the best thing that could have happened to me. I completely embrace it - and the fact that I'm a tried and true Capricorn. Boy did I get hit with a double whammy.

It's mild enough that's it's not immediately noticeable like a flashing billboard. I am usually able to function as someone who at first appears normal. As you get to know me, I start exhibiting signs of being quirky, anal, needing things done a certain way (by the way, there is only one way to do things and that's the right way), and not liking the idea of adapting to change.

Change is especially difficult for me when it's out of my control and I have to conform to it without prior notice. This happens at work a lot with our ever-changing underwriting and eligibility guidelines.

If something got fixed that wasn't broken and worked better before it was "fixed" then I all but lose it. Don't update my software to a system that functions worse than the last one causing me to operate less efficiently. I'll come into work and magically find that everything I've done for the past year has been turned on its ear and I have to learn how to do my job all over again. It can happen several times a year and I'm not the easiest person to work with on those days.

I mean several things when I say the only way to do things is the right way. One is that if you try something several times the same way and don't get the result you were aiming for, you're not doing something right. If it's not working, then stop doing it!

The other is where my OCD kicks in. I feel total empathy for anyone who suffers from this in a more extreme fashion than I do, but I can't understand how people are able to move on to something else if they know the first thing wasn't done to the best of their abilities. My OCD makes me do things in a very methodical, systematic way. My brain immediately scans every option I can think of in order to do something as efficiently as possible. Don't get me wrong. I can move on to other projects; I'm not saying I get stuck on something until I think it's a Picasso.

I mean that everything, absolutely everything, I can't stress enough that EVERYTHING you do has your name on it, put there by you with your stamp of approval. If you didn't do it to the best of your ability, why wouldn't you fix it? No one is perfect, and boy am I epitome of that statement but I do my personal best even if it's as simple as making a sandwich.

I completely embrace my OCD and don't know how I would get along in life if I didn't have it. I have a system for everything!

I buy Soy Milk, Almond Milk, and Cow Milk. If you take a look at the dates on unopened soy and almond milk you would see they are good for at least a month or two…until you open them.

Once they are opened, they go nasty within a week or less. My children are not permitted to open more than one type of milk at any given time. If I buy chocolate soy milk and regular or vanilla, they do not get to open another container until the first is finished. I will not be throwing away containers of chunky soy milk at $3.69 per container.

If they are headed to Daniel's house in a few days and it is his weekend, they won't be back for five days and I am allergic to soy. I can't drink it. It is a total waste to let them open something I will have to throw away before they get back because the container is swelling in my fridge.

This is all part of my system, one of my thousands of systems.

I am not a glass is half empty or half full kind of girl. I am, however, a dishwasher is only half full kind of girl.

That brings me to the "don't run my dishwasher" segment. My boyfriend thought he was helping me out by running the dishwasher before he left the other day. I knew there was so much more room to load all the dinner dishes when we got done eating that night and that was my plan.

After I was done cooking and eating with the girls, I started rinsing the dishes and prepping them to load into the dishwasher. I nearly lost it when I opened it to find it was half full of CLEAN dishes. Oh the humanity!

My mind went crazy. "No, he didn't. Please tell me he didn't." I checked the box of detergent knowing I had just cut the top open of the last box to get every last crumb of dust out of the bottom before I recycled it (I am laughing at my ridiculousness right now). The box in the cabinet was the new one standing by waiting to be opened.

I looked. The new one was opened. I was in a tizzy now. My whole system was thrown off for the entire evening. I schedule almost every minute and now I couldn't clean up from dinner until I first emptied my half clean dishwasher.

He thought he was helping, but had he not run the dishwasher I would have had exactly enough room to fill it with the dinner dishes and run it after the girls' showers. Then it would be clean by morning and I would empty it before work.

Did I mention that I had also just lost one load of detergent because he didn't maximize the space before he ran it? Don't even get me started on what the box looks like.

It comes with this neat little square sticker that if you take the time to do it right and peel if off slowly, doesn't rip the label or leave any remnants of sticker behind. Then I can neatly pull the metal spout out.

He tore it off! Now the paper is ripped and I have to look at this little torn piece of box until it is empty and this is a brand new box! I am going to have to look at this ripped box for over a month. If I hadn't already recycled the other box, I would have been found standing in my kitchen with a funnel trying to transfer the dishwasher detergent from the newer, torn box back into the old box.

Please feel free to laugh at me over my absurdness. He did. As soon as I realized he ran the dishwasher I texted him asking, "Did you run my dishwasher?" I knew the answer but asked anyway.

When he texted back, "I did, U mad?" I told him that I wasn't mad but that he was messing with my mojo. My face hurts from laughing at myself right now. I followed up by telling him that his actions had prompted me to add another chapter called, "Don't run my dishwasher!"

I got a text back, "No u didn't". He got a text back, "The heck I didn't".

So here is his part of the book that I promised him, entitled, "Don't run my dishwasher!"

Maybe I take what I do to extremes, but you can adjust what I do to fit what works for you. I just prefer to do things in a very particular, close to perfect way. I am far from perfect, but I do have awesome systems.

You should see how I make a bowl of oatmeal. It falls into that category I wrote about earlier about how you should do everything to the best of your abilities, even if it's something simple like making a sandwich. In this case, it's a bowl of oatmeal.

I make it really dry. That way when it comes out of the microwave too hot to eat, I can add an ice cube or just the right amount of cold water to give it the right consistency and temperature to eat without scalding my children's mouths. That way they can eat it faster rather than waiting for it to cool off when we are running late. Remember, that five minutes might make me late and I'm not going to have it.

I know I sound impossible, but Josh loves my crazy, quirky ways. When my OCD goes into overdrive my head involuntarily jerks to the side and my shoulder comes up to meet my ear like I have a cramp. I call it my "tick". Josh makes a game of it. In fact he thinks he's hysterical. I'll find the magazines slightly askew on my coffee table or he'll turn my coasters just enough that the corners don't meet properly so he can see how long it takes me to notice. In case you're wondering it takes me less than 10 seconds after I walk in the room. Don't get me started on what he does to the tube of toothpaste! I'll open the cabinet and find it squeezed in the middle! He'll switch my toilet paper so it flows under and not over. Uhhhgg!

Let me say this. I put as much effort and energy into all the good I do and the love I show everyone. Everyone else comes first. I do a lot for the people in my life to offset how compulsive and quirky I can be. I am equally as loving and reliable. It helps to keep the scales in balance.

Pay the Check

No one owes you anything...earn it

Earning. Now that's a word from history. I don't hear that one so much anymore. Why don't you help me dust it off and use it? Try it out, you might like it.

For some of you, it's going to be an acquired taste and for others, there will be no help for you. Unfortunately, you may be the more common type of person who feels like everything should be easy, served up and you'll be there for the delivery. If it's too much work, too much responsibility, you complain about why it isn't right for you, blame everyone but yourself and quit. Move on to the next job and it will turn out the same way because nothing is your fault and the world owes you just for showing up today. Get over yourself!

Earning was when people worked their fingers to the bone all day, in a job that wasn't beneath them, a job they might not have loved, or didn't make them feel fulfilled or ignite their passion. They worked those jobs because they had a family to feed and loved them enough to do it. They didn't seem to want for anything and lived happily with what they had. It's great if you get that passion and enjoyment from what you do, but if you have bills to pay and mouths to feed then you don't have the luxury of being picky.

Take what you can get, tighten the purse strings and put the fun on hold until you can afford to pay for it, AND the electric bill.

I love what I do but do you seriously think that I ran around as a child and said that I knew what I wanted to be when I grew up when someone asked, responding with, "I want to be an insurance agent when I grow up!" Uhhm, no, it wasn't quite like that.

I am very fulfilled with what I do thankfully, but not necessarily because I have the most fulfilling or rewarding career. My profession has been described as being one step up from a used car salesman but I make my job fulfilling and rewarding. To elaborate on the obnoxious comment and the smart-mouthed kid who passed it, I will tell you the same thing I told him. I first asked him if he stays in touch with his car salesman after he buys his car. For the used car dealer, the service ends with the sale. His job is done. For me, that is when my job begins. I am there all along the way, long after the purchase of the policy to protect the client through the years. My job doesn't end with the sale, that is where it begins, hence my expression, "The sale begins with the service". The fact that I'm successful at it and I make a good living helps, too. I look for ways to feel good about what I do and it's always right in front of me. I don't have to dig for it. I know I do a good job because I spend more holidays and birthdays with clients than I do family. I'm from out of town and it isn't always easy to travel to see family. How rewarding to receive multiple invitations on a regular basis to spend time outside of my office with clients and their families. I earned that through my genuine commitment to them and their needs. For me, that is extremely fulfilling.

I am not saying it's not okay to want nice things. I happen to have a true appreciation for shoes. I am 5"11" and don't give a hoot, I wear the big 4" heels, boots and strappies and I feel good wearing them. When people stare up at me as I walk by, I immediately follow their eyes right to my feet when they check to see if it's the heel or my height. I'll tell you it's both.

I just have a different perspective on how I choose which ones to buy this month or this year. If they really move me so much that I know I'll wear them for years and get enough use out them that they'll pay for themselves in wear, then I will get them so long as I like the price.

Do you know how long it's been since I bought myself a new pair of shoes? Gone are the days of buying the cute, every color shoe that I can only wear for one season with the one outfit they match, buying them with reckless abandon even though by the time I try the second shoe on the first one already hurts. No more convincing myself that they'll stretch or that they're cute enough for the pain. If you could see my feet now, you'd agree that no pain is worth what I've done to my toes.

Get rid of the attitude that world owes you something. Bring your hand back in and don't put it out again unless you're giving something to someone. Wait until you see how good it feels to earn something that you worked for that you can pay for with good ol' fashioned Benjamins, baby!

At about 8:45 last evening, I learned the lesson above in a profound and scary way. You know, the lesson about when things don't come easily, the easy thing to do is to walk away?

This book was relatively easy to write, but that's also before an editor has gotten their hands on it. That's beside the point. Last night I was very close to coming around the final stretch and finishing the book before I read and edited it.

I'm always careful to save my work a few times through my writing sessions and I wasn't that far into it last night. I had been typing for about an hour and got four pages done. The difference was, the four pages I typed were added all over the book in different chapters and they were added bits to the existing text.

My computer froze. Ok, it didn't really freeze, but I touched something. I was cutting and pasting a sentence and when I pasted it, that stupid little formatting box was blocking a few words that I couldn't read and it wouldn't go away. I double clicked on it to see if I could get it to disappear and a box opened. It was something about Word formatting, but the problem was, my little circle kept spinning and suddenly I was faced with "program not responding".

I lost everything because I hadn't saved anything for the hour that I had been there. Any data lost would be awful. I kept thinking that I would never remember all the little blurbs I had randomly inserted into chapters throughout the book. If I was going to lose data, this was NOT the data to lose.

If you're computer savvy, you're reading this and saying, Why didn't you just this….or why didn't you just that…?" I haven't a clue what I'm doing, that's why. I can turn the thing on and format a text box and get an Excel Spreadsheet to auto-sum. That is the extent of my computer knowledge. I panicked.

I spent hours last night clicking on recovery options, safe mode, and all the different options that Word was offering me. I could see three versions of my document in the left margin with time stamps on them. One was from 7:45 that morning which was the last time I had saved before I got ready for work. Two more had time stamps of 8:35pm and 8:45pm from before the circle began to spin.

I began to salivate. I got this wonderful message from Word that it had auto-saved and recovered my documents after telling me that a critical error happened last time I opened Word. It kept asking me if I wanted to continue. "Yes! I want to open it anyway! Give me my book!!!"

No matter what I did, the program wouldn't respond. Then the third document in recovery with the time stamp of 8:45pm disappeared. I was left with the two options from 7:45am which meant I lost everything I typed and the 8:35pm version. That 8:35 version now became so important to me figuring I could salvage the rest of what I typed in the last 10 minutes before I clicked that stupid formatting thingy.

I walked away to breathe. I smoked cigarettes. I ate oatmeal. I ate cookies. I smoked more cigarettes. I made a frenzied call to Josh then snapped at him because he made stupid suggestions to me about how to fix it. I tried anything I could to give the computer time to sort it out but my little circle kept spinning. I tried to restart but got the message that you have to force the restart because programs in the background are still open. If you force the restart all unsaved data will be lost. I am thankful for the cancel button. No restart just yet.

I prayed, really I did. I begged God to either magically restore my data, or give me the strength to start over. The thought of trying to remember four pages of inserted material seemed so hard and so unfair. I was usually so good about saving and this was the only time I hadn't. Why was I being punished? I knew this book was too good to be true. It had been too easy to write. How could I have written an entire book so easily in such a short period of time?

I almost threw my hands up and walked away. See how easy was it for me to face one small challenge and be ready to throw in the towel on 102 pages that were available me for me? Putting it into perspective, it would have been a whole lot worse if I lost the 102 pages and only had four, wouldn't it?

After some more time went by I was trying to sleep, and I kept praying. I told God that I knew this was the work of evil. He didn't want to see me succeed and I promised I wouldn't let that happen. I tried to go over the whole book and recall the pieces I had added. I texted Daniel just after it happened to tell him how beside myself I was. An hour later after I had cooled off, he called while I was tossing in bed.

He was facing a dilemma as well, and for the next hour and a half, I helped Daniel with his issue and all the while, gave myself the perspective on mine own, too. We had a good long conversation about good and evil and about not giving up, and I decided that I would be fine. After we got off the phone, I did the inevitable. I went out to the desk and forced the restart. I was tired and knew I had to face it in the morning.

I took my pen and pad to bed with me and every few minutes I'd pop the light on and jot something down that I was able to recall. I felt so much better because I decided not to give up when I was so close to the finish line.

The whole experience needed to go in the book because it is so relative to the very chapter I was about to write when I lost it all. I prayed again and thanked God for all I already had, prayed for the ability to remember as much as I could. I set my alarm an hour early to get the info back on the pages before I left for work. I don't normally pray for myself, but I thought an exception to the rule was in order and I thoroughly explained that in my prayers!

I didn't sleep very well and woke a few times throughout the night. At one point at about 1:20am, I gave it one last good old college try. I started the laptop with the hope that everything was there.

I couldn't look. I wouldn't let my eyes wander to the right side of the document telling me the time of the last update. I didn't want to see 7:45am yesterday. I still had hope.

I opened the document (which was stamped with 7:45am), sighed and went further to check for sure. When I opened the document my OCD kicked in and forced me save it again for whatever reason. Good ole OCD, saving a saved document. A lot of good that would do me, right?

Suddenly I saw this odd, unknown link that I hadn't seen before. It was something about compatibility mode, and it had options for me to retrieve other versions of the document. There were four or five choices, all time stamped from the day before and right before my eyes, was the 8:35pm version. I still lost the 8:45pm date but was never so happy to see 8:35 in front of me. Word had auto-saved at several different intervals of my work and I restored 90% of what I lost hours before. Yay Me!

At 1:20am I texted Daniel and Josh telling them both, "Score one more for God's team. He helped me recover 90% of what I lost, and I will remember the rest. Satan won't hold me down!" I added a little more to Josh's text and said I was sorry for freaking out on him earlier. I saved the document five more times and went back to bed.

I had a spiritual understanding of what was in front of me and felt I had really witnessed the battle of good vs. evil and I fought for the right side. I am on the right team. Doing the right thing was hard but oh it was so fulfilling. I had been rewarded for believing.

When I got up this morning, I put the cut-rate coffee on and fired up the laptop. Because this book became more important to me than the day before no matter how important it already was, I wanted to share it with you. I didn't give up. How silly would it have been to shelve this book over a few silly lost pages, but it proves the point I started making at the beginning of the chapter. It got hard and I was ready to give up. We're all guilty of it. I am guilty of it, too. If everything were easy we'd all be successful and we'd have it all. We have to work for it and earn it. I meant what I said earlier that the harder the challenge the more rewarding the result. If you hit a speed bump just accelerate once you're over it and you'll catch up in no time.

It's taking me longer to finish now because I am hitting save about every other paragraph or so but I don't care. I learned my lesson and don't want to make the same mistake twice. I'd rather save and re-save, check and re-check that I have done everything the right way and to the best of my ability than to make the same mistake and end up worrying like I did last night.

It was a small lesson in the big scheme of things but it was monumental for me because it was the difference of walking away from a goal I had set or staying to fight for what I want to accomplish.

I think a lot about what makes people tick sometimes and I wonder if we are the way we are to a certain extent because of how we're programmed. It's the debate of nature vs. nurture, or a little of both. I think our programming is the basis for how and why we act the way we do sometimes and the choices we make, but I am a firm believer that what we are taught impacts what we do with our original programming.

I'm not an optimist or a pessimist; I'm a realist. If you ask me if the glass is half empty or half full, I'm going to tell you it's neither. It's half a glass. What you make of it defines whether it's empty or full.

I have always had really hard-working values and they were further nurtured by how hard I saw my mother work and how my experiences growing up molded me. I haven't loved too many of the jobs I've held over the years but I've always done them as best I could.

I remember when I was about 24 years old I worked for a pizza shell company and I had to schlep a miniature 100-lb oven around in my car doing demonstrations on how to use our product. Sometimes they were done at food shows or tradeshows but many of them were held at restaurant supply warehouses.

On one particular day I was doing a demonstration at Restaurant Depot, baking pizzas and giving out samples along with product sheets, recipes, and instruction on how to use the product in different market places. It's an awesome product and I am still very good friends with the owners of the company. I could write a whole book about the trials and tribulations those two partners went through, both personally and professionally yet they kept at it. The company has seen great success and they have earned every bit of it.

On this particular day, I had just hauled that oven out of the back seat of my car, set everything up and waited for the little electric oven to hit 600 degrees. Plugging it in as soon as I got there was imperative because the product was really so good, people would start lining up to wait for the first slice as soon as I walked in. The oven took an hour to reach temperature and I was not about to hand out soggy, under-cooked, less-than-perfect pizza and ruin the reputation of the product or the company.

A tiny, little woman came barreling through the door like a burst of energy. She started exclaiming that she had heard I was here and wanted to make sure. I thought she was crazy and that she must have had me confused with someone else but she had me right. Her husband, a chef, had heard of our product. It was exactly what he had been looking for to put in their restaurant and he was coming in today to sample the product. I confirmed how long I was going to be there and what time I was wrapping up so he had the window to adjust his busy schedule to get there.

Sure enough this monster of a man approached shortly after and I spent an intense thirty minutes talking with him about what he could do with this product. He had as much energy as his wife and we covered every option, whether it was breakfast, grilled or barbequed pizza. You can put these shells on a barbeque and have the most delicious grilled pizza. After I showed him how to use the product, temperature, sauce and cheese to the edge, he wanted to buy a few cases to try.

I took him over to the freezer case where they were stored on the other side of the store. When I say freezer, I'm talking about a massive walk-in freezer the size of a small grocery store. I was not dressed to be in the freezer. Employees wore snowsuits with face-masks because it was so cold, but I didn't care. I walked right in, and started grabbing 35lb. boxes out of the cooler for him. He stopped in his tracks. He couldn't believe that not only did I NOT just lazily point in the direction of where they were, or walk him over to the general area. I went right in and started getting them for him. He was impressed with my efforts, not to mention my awesome ability to cook this specialty to perfection, and asked me if I would work for him.

He was opening a new restaurant in Northport, NY and thought I'd be perfect to help get this new product off the ground and train his staff on how to prepare them. Now I had two jobs. I'd work at the pizza shell company 9-5 and go right to the restaurant afterwards until it closed at 10pm. I didn't get out though, until 11pm when the place was spic-n-span. I was exhausted most days. I worked hard and didn't care that I wasn't the owner of either of these businesses. I worked as if I owned them and as if every dollar that came through the door was for me.

It turns out this was his second restaurant. I was working for one of the best chefs in New York and didn't know it. He was a crazy, self-taught chef who owned the #4 Zagat-rated restaurant on Long Island and he was intense to say the least. If you turned something less than perfect out to one of his customers, he'd let you know right in front of the entire restaurant.

He was known as the home of Grandma's Meatballs sold in enamel pots that you kept and brought back for refills. I worked there for two years until just before I married Daniel. Several months ago, I heard him on the radio. He had delivered meatballs to the Elvis Duran morning show in NYC and I listen every day on my way to work. I was freaking out! I tried to call the station at least ten times just so I could yell out, "I used to work for you!" I didn't get through.

Imagine my surprise when shortly after, I was watching the Food Network and caught an episode of Chopped. Guess who was the contestant on the show? My old boss from the restaurant! I learned so much from him, and I share this with you, because I busted my hump for so many years in jobs that didn't feel fulfilling or rewarding. It didn't matter. I had a job to do and I did it to the best of my ability. He used to joke that if I ever left the restaurant, he'd throw the pizza oven in the bay. That was rewarding. The bay was located right across the street from the restaurant. I went back several years later to see how he was doing and they weren't serving pizzas anymore. I can't help but feel it had something to do with me if only in a little, indirect way. That was pretty fulfilling.

He was really difficult to work for now and then, but he was pretty cool, too. He justified charging the prices he charged for his food because it was worth it. If you made it perfect then you could stand behind it and as long as the customer loved it, the price didn't matter. That's where my idea for the $12 book came from.

We had a meeting at work one night and he was going over menu changes. We were adding a simple salad to the menu. It was going to be $12 for this simple, little salad. We didn't care that he put the best greens, goat cheese, and dressing you could get into this salad. We just couldn't understand how he thought he would get away with charging $12 for a side salad.

He held up the salad after showing us the proper portion and how he wanted it made and said, "See? This is a $12 salad. Why? Because it's shiny." We all busted up laughing when he said that. Only he could make a comment like that make sense. That expression has stuck with Daniel and I for so many years that to this day, we use it for everything.

He calls me to tell me he had a $12 cleaning at the dentist and I know that his teeth are perfectly cleaned and shiny. When he asks if I had good service somewhere, I tell him I got $12 service and we both know that it means it was the best you could get.

You're not always going to love what you do or get the satisfaction you want from where you are in life, but remember, it can always be worse and no one owes you anything. When you get that sinking feeling on Monday morning or any morning that you don't want to return to the grind, think about what you're working for and appreciate what you have vs. what you don't have.

Daniel and I will sometimes talk and by the time the conversation is over, I know it's one of those days that I need to thank my boss for my job again. I am not talking about the schmoozing kind of insincere thanks. Every few months or so when I think my life stinks or that it's taking me so long to get anywhere, I look back to last year, a few years ago, or whenever and realize how far I've come. Sometimes you need to take a step back and look at the masterpiece you're creating to realize that even though it may not be near completion, you're still much further along than you were yesterday.

I go directly to my boss' office and tell him. "Hey Matt, I just want you to know that I appreciate working here, working for you, and being on your team." His face lights up. The first time I did this, he thought I was coming in to quit. I had to take a minute, just that one time to explain how my thought process works and that when my brain goes into overdrive, it makes me realize how good I really have it. Then it morphs into this feeling of wanting everyone who has anything to do with it, to know that I thank them and appreciate their part in making my life better.

I told you I have two influences to thank for my success. The first is God, whom I really thank every day and all throughout the day whenever things go my way, and the second is my boss for my employment. I said this more than once because it is that important to me. I have learned through my experiences that as soon as you don't appreciate something for what's it is worth, you run the risk of losing it. It is so easy to be thankful.

My boss gets a big kick out of it now when I thank him and returns it by telling me how much he appreciates having me work for him. We should be more thankful for the things we have. I am not saying to go searching these things out, but to open your eyes more and be aware that it's right in front of you. When you see it, stop and recognize your gratitude. Attitude is not everything but it is a huge part of it.

Good luck to you!

Leave a Tip

Other Books

I owe credit to some authors out there who have penned books that have impacted my life in a way that deserves telling them and letting you know about them as well. I want to take the unorthodox approach I told you about by crossing boundaries and giving credit where credit is due, no matter who the author is, or which publishing company it will benefit.

When I do something great for a client, I hope that client gives me a referral and tells someone that I'm worth a look. This is true of a few books I have read and I'd like to offer them a referral of sorts.

Love & Respect. This should be on the required reading list for all high school students before they are ever allowed to enter into a relationship. Many marriages, families, and relationships can be saved by what this book teaches.

I read it before Daniel. I read it two years ago and told him all about it. He didn't read it until very recently and made the saddest comment to me. He told me that the book was so awesome and that he could whole-heartedly relate to most of the stories in the book. He went on to say that had we known about and read that book years ago, it might have saved our marriage. He acknowledged that far too many times our egos got wound too tightly in the mix and he realizes now that all I ever really wanted was unconditional love and that all he ever really wanted was unconditional respect. Neither one of us gave each other what we needed because we both felt like we were owed something and were not willing to be the first to give it.

I recommend you read that book whether or not you are in a relationship. I am going to read it again because it's one of those books that no matter how many times you pick it up, you draw something different from it each time depending on your current situation.

365 Thank Yous. I received a tiny little book as a gift and at first made the mistake of "judging a book by its cover". I was almost a little insulted when I received it. I thought I was being targeted as someone who is not thankful and needed a lesson in etiquette. This is not that at all. It is such a heart-felt story packed with one of the most valuable lessons I've ever learned. Please consider reading, "365 Thank Yous".

The book was so infectious that I followed the guideline and wrote 365 thank you notes myself, as did my boss when I gave it to him to read. He didn't understand why I kept sending little notes. Then one day an underwriter from regional office sent him an email asking if he knew I had sent a ton of thank you cards to every one of the two hundred fire and auto underwriters in our company.

I hadn't told anyone what I was doing because that would take away from the purpose and make it insincere. The cat was out of the bag, and when I told him how profound this man's story was, he asked to borrow the book. We both went on to complete the task at hand. I received many cards back from my boss. My favorite was the last one because he sent me his 365th card to thank me for letting me know about that book. I'd like to let you know about it, too.

The Little Red Book of Selling. If you haven't already read it, I don't know what you're waiting for. It's not just about how to make great sales. Jeffrey Gitomer has already said a lot of the same things I stress in this book; we just have different ways of getting our points across. His book teaches you great habits to get into for a more successful life. It will help you with sales, but it is a book for everyone who needs improvement in their day-to-day lives. Although I had already practiced much of what I read, I realized that I had a lot more to learn from such an experienced person.

I had to empty my cup in order to make room to become the best I can be at what I do, and a great deal came from that little red book. In fact, I was moved to tell my story about the one bad experience I had at Kohl's because of a recent "Sales Caffeine" email I received from him about Carrabba's and his getting cheap bread. He and I have very similar views on customer service and how people deserve to be treated, though I am not intentionally making a comparison of myself to the great Gitomer!

This book was meant to help people as the books are that I mentioned above. I don't care where they came from or if it is considered a conflict to mention them. The whole purpose of sharing our experiences is to impart what we've learned unto others so that they may get the chance to better their lives. I hope this is true of you, too.

Don't Drive Yourself TOO Crazy

I realize that I sometimes take things to such an extreme that the end does not justify the means. I got tickets to see Pink for my birthday and I was so excited to be going away for the weekend. She was playing on Long Island, where I'm from, and I was really looking forward to seeing old friends and giving Josh a tour of where I grew up. When it came time to pack, I found myself in tears.

I tended not to notice little things on a daily basis that came to a head that evening. I wanted to take some nice things with me for the times we would go out to eat. I wondered what to wear for the concert. I had quite a little pity party the night before the trip. I should have been so excited to go, but I wasn't. My clothes were old. My shoes were old. I had no real luggage. I take really good care of my stuff in order for it to last until I can buy something new. Most days I look well put-together for work, but this was different. When it came time to pack a bag for the weekend, I became like a two year-old whining about having nothing new to bring. I buy such cheap stuff for myself that I allowed my mother to buy me a "luggage set" for Christmas that I thought would be good to use for a weekend away. It's a three-piece duffel bag set that would probably work for a two-night stay somewhere but we were going for four days. I put "luggage set" in quotes because when my mother was ordering it for me for Christmas, she asked me several times if it was REALLY what I wanted. Why? Because it was $16.95. Yup, $16.95 for a three-piece "luggage set". Add that to my worn clothes and shoes and within a half hour I was crying and throwing a hissy-fit. The type of hissy-fit I describe throughout the book when one whines why they have nothing.

I was angry with myself because I had seen some really nice REAL luggage on sale in good stores that would qualify as luggage, yet I refused to spend the money. Instead, I spent $50 on candles (there's money for whatever you want there to be money for) and decided I could do without luggage, shoes, a new pair of pants, or so much as a new top.

That's when I realized that perhaps I sometimes take things to too much of an extreme. My girls look like a million bucks with all new stuff and I feel like a pauper. I put myself in the position to play Martyr and not a very good one. I ranted all throughout the book that it's the trip that counts and the fact that I was fortunate enough to be going; yet there I was crying because my clothes were outdated. It probably wouldn't have bothered me as much if I had hair, but I'm bald right now. A week before the trip, I shaved my head COMPLETELY to raise money and awareness for childhood cancer. My hair hadn't grown back in yet so I was trying to pick feminine outfits to offset my baldness.

My point is that sometimes as human beings, we can't help but have desires and wants. It's ok to treat yourself to something nice once in a while and truthfully new clothes, if purchased within reason can sometimes be a need and not a want. I am not saying to run out and rack up bills buying stuff you don't need, but I have found myself on more than one occasion realizing that I've tripped over dollars to collect pennies, cut my nose to spite my face, or whichever cliché adage you want to pick.

I got the tickets for my birthday in December and the concert was in March, so it wasn't like it snuck up and bit me. I just had myself convinced that I needed nothing for the trip and whatever I had would make do. It wasn't until it was time to pack that reality set in and I found myself lacking. I will remember next time I am going somewhere to prepare ahead of time. I don't mind bringing my usual clothes with me, but if I know I'm going somewhere special, I will allow myself a reasonable purchase. Next time I earn some Kohl's cash from buying my collection of candles, I'll be sure to go back with it when the luggage is on sale again, use the Kohl's cash, and get my luggage almost free!

I'm not just human. I am a girl and as tough as I sometimes come across, there's a little girly-girl in there that fights to get out!

Afters
(For my British Friends)

Epilogue

I wrote this book in about two weeks. I started on Sunday, February 11, 2013, and today is March 1, 2013. I thought writing it was going to be the hard part, but I have started the editing and now realize how much more work needs to go into it before I can even consider begging someone to accept it for review for publication.

I want to clarify a few things even more so than I have throughout the book. I have beat on myself as well as others in order to get my point across. It is not my intention to make anyone feel bad about their choices or how they choose to live their lives. Ultimately what you do is up to you. I don't have to live with you or pay your bills, but I appreciate some good, healthy constructive criticism if it will help me improve. I tried to deliver it with a touch of humor that can in many cases, soften the blow of the harsh reality that truth hurts.

Along the way I have had many people point out where I can improve, how I can do something better, and what parts of me need an overhaul. I have had every delivery you can think of, from gentle heart-felt talks from important people in my life, to full-blown abusive rants from former bosses, friends, co-workers, anyone who has ever had issue with me. I remember all the lessons I've learned from the harsh to the kind and they have all helped me improve. I can tell you I am left with a much higher feeling of gratitude and respect towards the people who took the time to tell me in a kind or humorous way vs. the people who knocked me down and left me feeling less than worth-while. Keep this in mind when you go through life, and I wish you all best in your endeavors.

I hope you enjoyed my book, and perhaps I'll get the opportunity to give you something else to read in the future.